Star Quality

'This enchanting comedy, brilliantly adapted by Christopher Luscombe. A tough, elegant, hilariously observant light comedy of backstage life.' John Peter, *Sunday Times*

'An unexpected treat. The absurdities, vanities and fierce egotistical rivalries of the theatrical profession are deftly caught in a piece that manages to be both jaundiced and affectionate about its subject. A persuasive portrait of British theatre before the Royal Court revolution.' Charles Spencer, *Daily Telegraph*

'This crisp, vicious and very enjoyable play.' Robert Gore-Langton, *Daily Express*

'Hugely enjoyable.' Benedict Nightingale, *The Times*

'A biting backstage comedy – so just, wise and funny.' Michael Coveney, *Daily Mail*

Star Quality

Noël Coward was born in 1899 in Teddington, Middlesex. He made his name as a playwright with *The Vortex* (1924), in which he also appeared. His numerous other successful plays included *Fallen Angels* (1925), *Hay Fever* (1925), *Private Lives* (1933), *Design for Living* (1933) and *Blithe Spirit* (1941). During the war he wrote screenplays such as *Brief Encounter* (1944) and *This Happy Breed* (1942). In the fifties he began a new career as a cabaret entertainer. He pubished volumes of verse and a novel (*Pomp and Circumstance*, 1960), two volumes of auto-biography and four volumes of short stories: *To Step Aside* (1939), *Star Quality* (1951), *Pretty Polly Barlow* (1964) and *Bon Voyage* (1967). He was knighted in 1970 and died three years later in Jamaica.

Christopher Luscombe began his career writing and performing for the Cambridge Footlights. After five years of rep, he appeared in *Kean* at the Old Vic, and then joined the Royal Shakespeare Company, staying for seven years and playing a wide variety of parts. More recently he has appeared at the Royal National Theatre, Chichester Festival Theatre, toured with Oxford Stage Company and starred in *Art* at the Whitehall Theatre. His one-man show, *Half Time*, has been seen at the Donmar Warehouse, and *The Shakespeare Revue*, which he co-devised and directed for the RSC, has played in the West End and continues to tour in the UK and abroad.

Noël Coward's

Star Quality

Adapted by Christopher Luscombe

Methuen Drama

Published by Methuen 2001

3 5 7 9 10 8 6 4 2

First published in 2001 by
Methuen Publishing Limited,
215 Vauxhall Bridge Road, London SW1V 1EJ

Revised edition published in 2002

Copyright © 1967 The Estate of the late Noël Coward
Adaptation © 2001 Christopher Luscombe
Introduction © 2001 Sheridan Morley

Methuen Publishing Limited Reg. No. 3543167

A CIP catalogue record for this book is available from the British Library

ISBN 0 413 77145 8

Typeset by SX Composing DTP, Rayleigh, Essex
Printed and bound in Great Britain by
Cox & Wyman Ltd, Reading, Berkshire

Introduction

Of all the plays of Noël Coward (and there are around seventy, published and unpublished, produced and unproduced) *Star Quality* has perhaps the most complex history. It was first published as a short story in 1951; Noël himself later turned it into a play, but this version was only ever seen in a couple of Sunday night readings, one of which reopened the Theatre Royal Bath some twenty or so years ago.

Subsequently there were two television adaptations, one in America by William Marchant, and the other for the BBC by Stanley Price.

But it is only now, in late 2001, almost thirty years after Noël's death, that the actor and director Christopher Luscombe, working from Noël's original short story and then his largely unproduced script, has arrived at a version which at the time of writing is about to open at the Theatre Royal Windsor, at the start of a pre-West End tour, with Penelope Keith in the leading role.

Noël himself was always fascinated by the backstage world of theatre: in early poems such as 'The Boy Actor' and songs such as 'Why Must the Show Go On?' and of course the more familiar 'Mrs Worthington', as well as plays such as *Red Peppers* and *Waiting in the Wings*, he deals unsentimentally and often cynically with the roar of the greasepaint and the smell of the crowd. A child actor from the age of ten, Coward enjoyed a lifelong devotion to the theatre, and in his diaries and memoirs there are some of the best-ever descriptions of the changing theatrical world of the first half of the last century.

Star Quality also solves, for me at any rate, one of the few remaining Coward mysteries; when at his invitation I published his (and my) first biography back in 1969, we became close friends, and he became godfather to my son Hugo. One night, not long before he died in his beloved Jamaica in March 1973, we were discussing my book and the extraordinary amount of good luck it had brought to both him and me. 'There is though,' said Noël, 'just one little

problem with it. You describe me all through the book as this
rather lonely, even isolated figure, and to your generation
that is how I must seem. But you have to remember that I
started out as half of a double act.'

He meant, of course, with Gertrude Lawrence: they met as
child actors on Euston Station in 1913; 'she gave me an
apple', Noël noted, 'told me a few mildly dirty stories, and I
loved her from then onwards'.

They toured as 'Wonder Children' all through the First
War. In the 1920s, his first great song hit, 'Parisian Pierrot',
was written for Gertie and introduced by her both in the West
End and on Broadway. In the 1930s, he wrote for her first
Private Lives and then the amazingly ambitious sequence of
nine plays and musicals (among them the original *Brief
Encounter*) known as *Tonight at 8.30.*

'I imagined,' said Noël later, 'that we would always be
acting together into our eighties or nineties.' But, as they say,
if you want to make God laugh, you tell Him your plans.
What happened was that Gertie settled in America, the War
came, and she married her theatre manager up on Cape Cod.

So by 1945, Noël and Gertie were separated by the War,
by the Atlantic and by her marriage. In the following year,
she went out to Hollywood to film a curiously terrible version
of Tennessee Williams' *The Glass Menagerie*, in which she
plays, somewhat implausibly, a Southern belle with a strong
south London accent.

While there, however, Gertie saw Rex Harrison and Irene
Dunne in a movie called *Anna and the King of Siam*, and realised
at once that here could be a musical for her. She persuaded
Rodgers and Hammerstein to write it as *The King and I*, in the
vague hope that Noël might consent to play the King.
Coward declined, on the grounds that he hated long runs,
didn't like New York in summer, and disliked singing other
people's songs, however good.

Instead he recommended a young, unknown friend, Yul
Brynner, and the rest is musical-theatre history. Except that
during the run Gertie's health began to give out, along with
her voice; Rodgers and Hammerstein wrote to Noël asking if,
for the good of her health and their show, he could persuade

her to leave the cast. Gertie refused. She had never given up before, and she wasn't about to start now.

Besides, she had one great dream left: she wanted to come home to England for the Coronation summer of 1953 and play *The King and I* at Drury Lane; after fifteen years abroad, a royal return home. She feared, moreover, that if she left the show on Broadway, she would forfeit that chance. So she played on through the long, hot summer of 1952 and in September Noël went racing at Folkestone, backed a few winners, came off the course, bought an evening paper and was stunned to read in the stop press GERTRUDE LAWRENCE DEAD. She was just 54, and it was cancer.

Almost unable to see for tears, Noël went home and wrote her obituary for *The Times*: 'No one I have ever known, however gifted, meant what she meant to me and my work. Her quality was to me unique, and her talent imperishable.'

Twenty years later, idiotically, I once asked Noël if he still ever thought about her: 'Every night before I go to sleep,' he replied, 'and every morning when I wake up, I see her in that white Molyneux dress on that terrace in *Private Lives*, and she never goes away.'

The last thing Noël asked me to do was to write her biography, which I did under the title *A Bright Particular Star*. I also wrote a show called *Noël & Gertie* (in America, *If Love Were All*) in which such varied and blazing stars as Patricia Hodge, Twiggy and Susan Hampshire have all been my Gerties.

But the curious thing was that when I searched through Noël's own memoirs, his diaries and his letters, I could find very little on Gertie. Occasional outbursts of rage at her ingratitude, her first reaction to *Private Lives* ('Nothing wrong that can't be fixed'), and the brief, heartbreaking obituary, but that was more or less that.

Until, of course, I read *Star Quality* and found there the best description of Gertie ever. This is not to say by any means that the whole character of Lorraine is based on her, and indeed there are aspects of Lorraine's character which would be a better match for such other long-time Coward players as Lynn Fontanne or Margaret Leighton.

But in what is now Bryan's long curtain speech about

Lorraine there is an absolute, precise and detailed description of Gertie for better and for worse, a woman whose 'whole life is passed in a sort of hermetically sealed projection room watching her own rushes'.

Unlike Noël, Gertie left very little behind: a few scratchy recordings, four or five movies in which she was less than wonderful, and the memories of pre-war theatregoers who alas are now dying off very rapidly indeed. But she lives on in that last speech, and what she had of course, as Noël writes, was 'quality – star quality'.

Sheridan Morley
July 2001

(Sheridan Morley wrote the biographies of Noël and Gertie, which are now published in one paperback volume by Oberon as *Private Lives*. His authorised biography of Sir John Gielgud was published by Hodder & Stoughton. He is drama critic of the *Spectator* and the *International Herald Tribune*.)

Adaptor's Note

In 1999, the centenary of his birth, Noël Coward seemed to take over my life. Firstly, I found myself at Chichester Festival Theatre playing Beverly Carlton, the part famously based on Coward, in Kaufman and Hart's *The Man Who Came to Dinner*. This involved spending several weeks listening to tapes and watching videos, working on an impression of a man whose voice and delivery is still so familiar. As Kenneth Tynan put it in 1953, 'even the youngest of us will know, in fifty years' time, exactly what we mean by "a very Noël Coward sort of person".' I was painfully aware that the audience at Chichester would certainly know.

Then an offer came to co-devise a new Coward revue, *Masterpieces* (which is currently in preparation). This encouraged me to continue my study of Coward's work. I hadn't realised quite how prolific he was, and found all kinds of unexpected delights amid the lesser-known material – the poetry, the diaries, the autobiographies and the short stories. Among the latter was *Star Quality*, a memorable tale of theatre folk behaving badly.

I'm fortunate to share a literary agent with the Coward Estate, and this gave me easy access to the unpublished work. I came across several photocopied manuscripts, among them a playscript of *Star Quality*, written between 1966 and 1967, and hitherto unproduced. It was intriguing to see how Coward envisaged a stage version of his story, but the play is quite an epic, with eighteen speaking parts, three acts and numerous locations. I began to see why no commercial management had leapt to produce it! And the play inevitably diluted the short story, in which Coward, free of censorship, had been able to conjure up a rather more authentic account of the language and leanings of the theatrical profession.

So what I have tried to do in my adaptation is to pare down the script, remove the extraneous characters, suggest a more fluid style of presentation and keep to the spirit of the short story. I have been greatly helped in this by the generosity of Graham Payn and the Coward Estate.

I must also record my gratitude to a number of friends who

have put up with me over the last year or so, when I seemed increasingly to resemble *Star Quality*'s hapless hero, the writer Bryan Snow. They read the various drafts and gave me invaluable advice: Hugh Bonneville, Debra Gillett, Rob Howell, Penelope Keith (who, I'm delighted to say, eventually created the leading role), Brigid Larmour, Malcolm McKee, Sam Mendes, Lesley Moors, Mary Roscoe, Al Senter, Matthew Warchus and especially James Barber of Guildford's Yvonne Arnaud Theatre, who commissioned the script and effectively became the godfather of the first production. I am also indebted to Bill Kenwright and all his colleagues, and to the original cast, who contributed so much to the final draft.

Christopher Luscombe
August 2001

Star Quality

Star Quality was first performed at the Theatre Royal Windsor on 7 August 2001, transferring to the Apollo Theatre, Shaftesbury Avenue, on 23 October. It was presented by Bill Kenwright Ltd., and the cast was as follows:

Bryan Snow, *Author of* Dark Heritage	Nick Fletcher
Ray Malcolm, *Director of* Dark Heritage	Russell Boulter
Nora Mitchell, *Lorraine Barrie's maid-cum-dresser*	Marjorie Yates
Lorraine Barrie, *Eleanor in* Dark Heritage	Penelope Keith
Harry Thornton*, *Stage Manager*	Graham Ashe
Beryl Fletcher*, *Assistant Stage Manager*	Fiz Marcus
Bob Deacon*, *Assistant Stage Manager*	Andrew Coppin
Eric Larch, *Aubrey in* Dark Heritage	Magnus Hastings
Marion Blake, *Stella in* Dark Heritage	Una Stubbs
Gerald Wentworth, *Mortimer in* Dark Heritage	Peter Cellier
Laura Witby*, *Elise in* Dark Heritage	Helen Dorward
Tony Orford, *Ray Malcolm's Personal Assistant*	Nick Waring

Director Christopher Luscombe
Designer Tim Goodchild
Lighting Designer Rick Fisher
Sound Designer Wayne Cross
Fight Director Malcolm Ranson

The play is set in London, Kent and Manchester during the summer of 1951.

The text is adapted from Noël Coward's 1951 short story and his unproduced 1967 play, both entitled *Star Quality*.

*These roles are non-speaking, and can be played by the real stage management if necessary.

Act One

Scene One

The stage is empty apart from a few items of furniture which we can just make out in the gloom. As the houselights go down, a door opens right at the back of the stage. **Bryan Snow** *enters in a shaft of light. He is in his late twenties and carries a script. He closes the door and walks down to the footlights. He looks around, up into the flies and out into the auditorium. Another figure enters –* **Ray Malcolm**. *He's about ten years older than* **Bryan** *and is smoking a cigarette. He addresses* **Bryan** *across the darkness.*

Ray   You are sure you want her, aren't you, Bryan?

Bryan   Yes. Yes, I am.

Ray   You believe she's got it in her?

Bryan   Why? Don't you?

Ray   I'm asking you.

Bryan   Well . . . yes, I do.

Ray   Has she read it?

Bryan   She's had the script for a fortnight, and apparently she wants to meet me.

Ray   Good. (*He smiles at him.*) It's up to you then.

Bryan   Me?

Ray   You'll be all right. Actors love to meet the author. It makes them feel they're being taken seriously. Anyway, she'll eat you up with a spoon.

Bryan   I don't know what makes you think that, I'm –

Ray (*suddenly steely*)   But you've got to get her to commit.

Bryan   Right.

Beat.

Do you happen to know if she gets on with Gerald Wentworth?

Ray   As well as she does with any leading man; a little better if anything. They had a bit of a swing round the first time they worked together – but that was long before the War; since then they've teamed up once or twice fairly painlessly. I'm sure she drives him mad, but for a year or two in the West End he'd put up with anything, even Lorraine Barrie.

Bryan   You do know an awful lot about her.

Ray   I like to do my homework.

Bryan   Did I tell you I was at the first night of *Waters of the Moon,* and caught a glimpse of her down in the stalls. She was looking wonderful.

Ray   She always looks wonderful.

Bryan   Perhaps you'd like to come with me when I meet her.

Ray   God, no. I'll have quite enough of her later on. There's one thing I'm certain about though. (*He chucks away his cigarette end and grinds it into the floor.*) I know I can deal with her.

Bryan   What makes you so sure?

Ray   One very good reason. Despite everything, despite all the tantrums and traumas, she's a bloody good actress, and she knows it as well as I do. She also knows that I can get a first-rate performance out of her, which is all she really cares about. But before I can do that, she's got to say yes.

Bryan   Of course. (*He opens his script.*) I did wonder if I could just ask you a couple of things about the script.

Ray (*with a hint of impatience*)   No. Not now. Just put your mind to hooking our leading lady.

Bryan   Yes.

Beat.

But you do think the new draft is on the right track, don't you, Ray?

Ray (*shrugging*)   It's fine. Just get her.

He leaves.

Bryan *is left on his own feeling slightly deflated. He wanders over to a large easel which is covered by a light dust sheet. He tentatively pulls off the sheet, and as he does so, sunlight floods the room and music creeps in.*

It's about five o'clock on a fine summer afternoon, and we can now see that we're in the drawing room of **Lorraine Barrie**'*s mews house in Knightsbridge. This is a home which could belong to no one but a famous actress or a set designer. The room (suggested simply by the furniture) is dominated by the impressive oil painting of* **Lorraine** *which sits on the easel. She is shown in the portrait sitting before her dressing room mirror staring fixedly at herself. Behind her chair, and also reflected in the mirror, is her maid-cum-dresser,* **Nora Mitchell**.

Scene Two

Nora *enters wearing a discreet black dress and white apron, looking exactly as she does in the painting. She's a laconic woman of a certain age, apparently unimpressed by the world she inhabits. The music fades.*

Nora   Miss Barrie won't be more than a few minutes, so make yourself comfortable.

Bryan   Thank you.

Nora (*indicating a box*)   There are cigarettes if you want to smoke.

Bryan   No thank you. Not just yet.

Nora   I'll go and fetch the tea tray. Miss Barrie always likes to pour it herself. She makes quite a production of it as a matter of fact. Having had to do it so often on the stage it's become second nature to her. In *Wise Man's Folly* she poured out no fewer than one thousand four hundred and seventy-two cups of tea and ate seven hundred and thirty-six sandwiches.

Bryan   Good heavens!

Nora   And that doesn't include rehearsals and the three week try-out in Liverpool.

Bryan   She must have got awfully sick of them.

Nora   She did. So we'd try and ring the changes. Joe, the prop man, and me, we used to put our heads together.

Bryan   Did that help?

Nora (*ignoring the interruption*)   We'd do caviar one night, chopped egg the next, then a nice bit of gammon and so on.

Bryan   I see.

Nora   Once we tried Lyle's Golden Syrup as a surprise. But it was too runny and got all over her frock, which didn't go down very well.

Bryan   Luckily there's no eating in my play!

The telephone rings.

Nora   Excuse me.

She goes to the telephone. **Bryan** *stands aside tactfully.*

(*At telephone.*) Hello. Yes, this is Miss Barrie's residence. No, I'm afraid you can't at the moment, she's in conference. Oh it's you, Miss Blake! I never recognised your voice. No, I really can't disturb her now. She's talking to the author of the new play. (*She winks at* **Bryan**.) Oh yes – seems very nice . . . Right, I'll tell her you called . . . Well, you might catch her at about seven before she goes out, or if not you'd better try in the morning. Bye-bye for now. (*She hangs up.*) That woman's a pest. (*She looks at him.*) Marion Blake.

Bryan   Ah.

Nora   Always badgering Miss Barrie about something or other. I can't think why she puts up with her – all that gush.

Bryan   Would you say she's a good actress?

Nora   All right in a small part; but give her a big scene to play and she's murder. She understudied Miss Barrie years ago in *Bold as Brass* and had to go on for a Thursday matinée. It was a killer. She's one of them gaspers.

Bryan   Gaspers?

Nora   You know, gets all breathless in the emotional bits and cries herself to a standstill. We thought she'd had an asthma attack. She'll go to town in that part you've got her down for.

Bryan   Which part?

Nora (*as if stating the obvious*)   Stella.

Bryan   Oh, I don't think that's quite settled yet. You've read the play then?

Nora   Of course. I read all Miss Barrie's scripts.

Bryan   Did you . . . did you like it?

Nora   It's not my place to say whether I liked it or not.

Bryan   No; but I should certainly welcome your opinion.

Nora   Well, if you really want to know what I think, you're going to find yourself in trouble with that last act.

Bryan (*defensively*)   Most people who read it seem to think Act Three's the best.

Nora   Oh, it reads all right. It's when they start acting it that I'm talking about.

Bryan (*getting a little anxious*)   Does Miss Barrie think this too?

Nora   I don't know. We haven't discussed it.

Bryan   She must be interested in your opinion if she asks you to read her scripts.

Nora   It's not so much that she asks me to read them; she just leaves them lying about.

Bryan (*slightly put out*)   Oh.

Nora   Anyway, I wouldn't worry about it now. That's what try-outs are for, aren't they? But take my advice and have your typewriter handy when you get to Manchester.

Bryan (*still ruffled*)   Yes, but what exactly do you think is wrong with the last act?

Nora   Well . . . I just don't think you'd ever get her to do it.

Bryan   I'm sorry – do what?

But before **Bryan** *can have his mind put at rest, the door opens and* **Lorraine Barrie** *comes swiftly into the room. She is an exceedingly attractive woman in her late fifties, but of course looks a good deal younger than that. She is obviously and unmistakably a star, which means that over and above her natural good looks she has great vitality and an air of assurance acquired from years of indiscriminate adulation. She is wearing grey linen slacks, a lime-coloured sports shirt and enormous dark glasses. In her left hand she carries a blue-covered typescript and in her right, a small Aberdeen terrier.*

Lorraine   Look! (*She waves the script triumphantly at* **Bryan**.) You've come at exactly the right moment. I was just reading your wonderful play for the seventh time! (*Handing the dog to* **Nora**.) Nora darling, be an angel and take Bothwell from me – he's getting restless and we all know what that means. Pop him out into the mews. And we'll have the tea now. (**Nora** *takes the dog out.*) He's called Bothwell because Paul Martin gave him to me when I was playing Mary Stuart in Newcastle. As a matter of fact, I don't believe Mary Stuart herself got much further than Newcastle, did she?

Bryan   I'm not really sure.

Lorraine   Poor creature. I enjoyed playing her up to a point, but she was a cracking fool. Never put a foot right from the word go. I always think she and Marie Antoinette were two of the silliest women in history.

Bryan   Well, they certainly paid for it.

Lorraine   But they needn't have if only they'd had just a smidge of common sense. I wear these dark glasses when I meet people for the first time because I'm fundamentally a very shy person and they give me a sense of security, but now that I've seen what you're like I don't feel shy any more, so I'll take them off. (*She does so.*) There – that's better.

Bryan (*looking at the portrait, after a slight pause*)   What a wonderful painting.

Lorraine   It's a Charles Donovan. He did it before the War. Personally I loathe it, but it's supposed to be one of the best things he ever did.

Bryan (*weakly*)   He's certainly caught you awfully well.

Lorraine   It's really better of Nora than it is of me. Look at the way he's done the hair just on the point of collapse, and the painting of the hands and that heavenly safety pin! It's terrifying, isn't it? I need hardly say that she despises it. She says it makes her look like a lavatory attendant, and of course I've never had the heart to tell her that that's exactly what she does look like. Do sit down and relax.

She sits in the armchair and **Bryan** *perches, with desperate care, on the edge of the sofa.* **Nora** *returns without Bothwell but with the tea tray which she places on the coffee table.*

Nora   Miss Blake called.

Lorraine   Oh Lordy.

Nora   I told her to try again round about seven.

Lorraine   Poor Marion. Was she in one of her states?

Nora (*dourly*)   She sounded much the same as usual.

Lorraine (*to* **Bryan**)   Marion Blake is an old, old friend of mine, but I'm afraid she does live on her nerves. Do you know her?

Bryan   No, we've never met.

Nora   That's a treat in store for you.

Lorraine   Go away, Nora, if you can't be nice.

Nora *shoots her a look and goes out.*

Lorraine   I couldn't live without Nora. She's been with me since I was at the Haymarket, long before the War. Which dates us both, now I come to think about it. This is China tea. If you prefer Indian there's masses in the kitchen and you can have a little pot all to yourself.

Bryan   No, China's perfect thank you.

Lorraine (*pouring the tea*)   You know, you're quite different from what I thought you'd be. I can't imagine why but I expected someone much older and drier. In fact I can tell you now I was really quite nervous. I've always had a dreadful inferiority complex about authors. To me there's something incredible about people being able to sit down and write plays and books. It's torture to me to have to write so much as a postcard.

Bryan   I find postcards difficult myself.

Lorraine   I'm just physically incapable of stringing three words together on paper. I suppose it's never having been to school properly. I'm completely uneducated, you know.

Bryan   That's very hard to believe.

Lorraine   It's true – I swear it. I used to drive poor Doodie Rawlings quite frantic when he directed me. In *The Cuckold of Eastcheap*. Doodie's an Oxford don with a passion for the theatre –

Bryan   Yes, I know.

Lorraine   Of course you do. Well, he was astounded that anyone in the world could be as ignorant as me.

Bryan   I bet you knew more than he did about the theatre.

Lorraine   God knows I ought to. I've been at it since I was seven.

Bryan   Seven?! What were you playing?

Lorraine   Mamillius in *The Winter's Tale*. (*Simply and tenderly.*) 'A sad tale's best for winter. I have one of sprites and goblins . . .'

Bryan   Where was that?

Lorraine (*breaking the spell*)   The Palace, Manchester, back in Nineteen Hundred and Frozen to Death. (*She hands him a cup of tea.*) I don't know whether you like sugar or milk or neither so just help yourself. I made those little scones myself specially for you, so you must eat them all up to the last crumb. I adore baking, but I never dare go into the kitchen when Nora's in the house, so I send her off to the pictures every so often and have a real field day. Do you cook?

Bryan   Only scrambled eggs, I'm afraid.

Lorraine (*with moving sincerity*)   There's nothing in the world more divine than scrambled eggs. Particularly if you mix in some of that rather common-looking pink caviar you can get at Fortnum's. It's a bit salty, but it zips them up no end.

Bryan   It sounds wonderful. I'll try it.

Lorraine   Tell me about this new man who's directing the play: Ray Something-or-other.

Bryan   Ray Malcolm.

Lorraine   Yes. I missed the thing he did at Hammersmith and wild horses wouldn't drag me to Stratford, particularly with poor Etta Marling flogging her way through Cleopatra, so I've never really seen any of his work at all.

Bryan (*aware of a sudden uprush of feeling*)   That's a pity beacause he's quite extraordinary. A truly first-class mind.

Lorraine (*assuming an expression of grave interest*)   But does he really know about the theatre? Or is he one of those bright sparks who pop out of the Services, bursting with theories and doing endless productions of *Murder in the Cathedral*?

Bryan   No, I wouldn't say that. The way he talks about the play always makes me think that it would be wonderful to be directed by him. I've done a little acting myself, you see.

Lorraine   Good for you. Where?

Bryan   Aldershot. During the War. I don't really think I was cut out for it, but meeting Ray made me long to have another go. I almost thought of suggesting myself to play the boyfriend.

Lorraine (*unable to conceive of the young man before her as boyfriend material*) What fun!

Bryan   But he'll have someone else in mind, I expect, and anyway I'm probably not quite the right type. (*Aware of the need to get the conversation back to* **Lorraine**.) The other day in the producer's office he was praising you to the skies.

Lorraine   Was he indeed.

Bryan   Yes. He said that your talent was clear and true and that you had a particular magic of your own that no other living actress possessed.

Lorraine   And did your producer agree with him, or say that I was a monster?

Bryan (*before he can stop himself*)   Both.

Lorraine (*laughing, and offering* **Bryan** *another scone*)   J.C. adores me really, but he's always telling people that I'm impossible because I won't stand for any of his nonsense. And I've never quite forgiven him for his behaviour over *Monkey Puzzle*.

Bryan   What did he do?

Lorraine   Fired Maureen Raleigh on the spot and brought in Barbara Copeland the week before we opened! Without even discussing it with me!

Lorraine *has poured herself some more tea and now waves the teapot enquiringly at* **Bryan**, *who holds out his cup.*

Bryan   Without consulting you? That's incredible. But what did you think of Barbara Copeland? (**Bryan** *is a fan.*) Isn't she –

Lorraine   All gong and no dinner. (*She puts the teapot down with a crash.*) Dreadful! And to cap everything, the critics, who are incapable of telling the difference between a good part and a good actress, gave her rave notices! I don't think I have ever been so deeply angry in my whole life. And I've never quite forgiven J.C. for that. His behaviour killed something in me – do you know what I mean? It isn't that one wants to go nursing grievances. One wants to make up and be friends – and forget. But there are some things one just can't forget. After all it wasn't myself I was thinking of – it was the play! That's where I'm such a fool, but I can't help it. I always put the play first. To me the author is sacred.

Bryan   My goodness, Miss Barrie, if I were lucky enough to be your author and you treated me as sacred, well, I'd die of embarrassment.

Lorraine *goes over and sits next to* **Bryan** *on the sofa. She looks at him intently for a moment. When she speaks the whole timbre of her voice changes, and with it her whole personality. It's as though the light in the room has been lowered.*

Lorraine   I want you to promise me something here and now. I want you to promise me that if I were to say yes –

and I'm really not sure that I can – but if I were to say yes, you would always be absolutely and completely honest with me. What star sign are you?

Bryan   Capricorn.

Lorraine   Yes, I thought so. I have a strange feeling that we are friends even though we have only just met. I have the advantage of you, of course, because whereas you have never known me before, I have known you. I have learnt to know you and become fond of you through your lovely, lovely play . . .

Bryan   Please, Miss Barrie, I –

Lorraine   Don't say anything for a moment, my dear. Let me finish. I have never been good at paying extravagant compliments, particularly to anyone whom I respect. But I want to tell you frankly now, that this agonising, twisted, moving play of yours is one of the most beautiful things I have ever read, and I can only swear solemnly that, if I did take it on, I would do my very best to prove worthy of it.

She flashes **Bryan** *a brave smile, and he is startled to see that her eyes are filled with tears. The telephone rings.*

(*With a change of mood as sudden as a slap in the face.*) Damn it! I told Nora I didn't want to be disturbed. (*Into the receiver.*) Hello! Who is it?! Clemmie dear, I meant to have called you before but Bryan Snow is here and I got so carried away talking about the script that I completely forgot what the time was. (*To* **Bryan***, her hand over the receiver.*) My agent. (*Back into receiver.*) Yes, darling, of course I do. I think you might have warned me that he was young and attractive and has a divine sense of humour. (*She blows* **Bryan** *a kiss.*) I expected somebody middle-aged and starchy and difficult, and was prepared to tear myself to shreds in order to make him approve of me – Yes, of course he does. (*She smiles roguishly at* **Bryan***.*) You do approve of me, don't you?

Bryan (*wondering if this is the beginning of a love affair*)   You know I do. I think you're wonderful.

Lorraine (*back into receiver*)   What news from J.C.'s office?

She tucks her feet up under her and becomes completely involved in the conversation, forgetting that **Bryan** *is in the room.*

Have they got anyone to play Stella yet? What about Marion Blake? . . . In heaven's name, why not? . . . Never heard such nonsense in my life! She's one of the best little actresses we've got . . . Oh, so it was Ray Malcolm who turned her down, was it? I see. And who does he suggest? . . . Carole Wylde?! Must be out of his mind. (*Catching sight of* **Bryan**.) Hold on a minute. (*She puts her hand over the receiver and turns to* **Bryan**.) Your Mr Thingummyjig wants Carole Wylde to play Stella.

Bryan (*apprehensively*)   Yes, I know he does.

Lorraine   Have you ever *seen* Carole Wylde?

Bryan   Only once, in *Leave Me My Heart.* I have to say I thought she was rather effective.

Lorraine   You can't possibly go by that. It's a foolproof part. She couldn't *begin* to play Stella. She's far too young, and that maddening voice would drive people out of the theatre. Always sounds as if she were gargling.

Bryan   Yes, but in a way –

Lorraine (*back into receiver*)   Listen, Clemmie, you can tell Mr Whatever-his-name-is that he'll have to think again. I wouldn't dream of playing that crucial scene in the last act with Carole Wylde; she's totally wrong for it . . . Yes, dear, I know the critics are potty about her, and I daresay she won a gold medal at the RADA, but if she plays Stella she'll be playing it without me. The part cries out for Marion Blake. . . . I can't help whether he likes her or not. And you can tell J.C. from me that I consider it very high-handed of him to engage a director that I've never even clapped eyes on . . . Very well, dear. Call me in the morning. I shall be in until lunchtime.

She replaces the receiver and sits silently for a moment with her eyes closed. After a pregnant pause she opens them again and holds out her hand. She speaks in a weary voice.

Give me a cigarette, just to calm me down, because that really has put me into the most terrible rage.

Bryan (*handing her a cigarette*)   Please don't be upset. (*He lights it for her.*)

Lorraine (*inhaling deeply*)   It's incredible – quite incredible.

Bryan   I don't think Ray is all that set on Miss Wylde. I'm quite sure that if you talked it over with him he'd see exactly what you mean.

Lorraine   He ought to know without my telling him that Carole Wylde in that part would throw the whole play out of kilter. That's what disturbs me – the fact that he needs to be told. I'm in despair. I really am. I don't think I can go through with all this.

Bryan   I'll talk to Ray this evening. I'm sure it will all be –

Lorraine   I blame J.C. He's not what I call a producer. He's a glorified estate agent. He's always getting idiotic crazes for 'exciting new talent' as he calls it. Do you remember Yvonne Laurie?

Bryan   No, I don't think I do.

Lorraine   Neither does anyone else. She was one of J.C.'s exciting new talents. He dragged her out of the provinces, where she was perfectly happy pottering about in small repertory companies, and gave her the lead in that French play that Edgar Price translated into basic Surbiton. She played a clapped-out Egyptian prostitute in chiffon trousers and an armful of slave bracelets. The play ran three nights.

Bryan   What happened to her?

Lorraine   One season at the Old Vic and then oblivion.

Bryan   There was once talk of *you* going to the Old Vic, wasn't there?

Lorraine (*shuddering*)   There certainly was – they've been hounding me for years – but I'd rather die. I'm too old and too tired. (*She sighs and gazes into the middle distance.*) I expect I'm too old-fashioned as well. I've been at the game too long. I learnt the hard way. Now everything's different. Amateurs have taken possession of the theatre. Take this young director that you're all so mad about. Where did he learn his trade?

Bryan   I think he was running a repertory company in Yorkshire when he was called up.

Lorraine   I've nothing against rep, nothing against it at all. He may be a genius for all I know. But this play of yours doesn't need genius, it has that already in the writing. What it does need is a real down-to-earth professional to direct it, a man with all the technical tricks at his fingertips. God preserve us from enthusiastic amateurs like Doodie Rawlings who have ghastly theories about acting and witter on about rhythm and colour.

Bryan   I did think his *Hamlet* was rather exciting.

Lorraine   All that unbleached calico? The closet scene looked like a tea-tent on Derby Day.

Bryan   You must admit the lighting was superb.

Lorraine   I admit no such thing. He lights the scenery, not the actors. Poor Rita Devon had more lines on her face than she had in the script. But let's not argue. You obviously share the general opinion that Ray Malcolm is the new Messiah. I'm merely reserving judgement. But of this I do assure you: I always go into rehearsals with an absolutely open mind. I'm sure that Ray is brilliant. But you are the one, to me, who really counts.

Bryan   You're very kind, Miss Barrie –

Lorraine   Please! 'Lorraine'. We're friends now. Friends and allies against a common foe.

Bryan   I really don't think we should look on Ray as an enemy.

Lorraine   That was a joke. Actually I can't wait to meet him. (*She stands, and* **Bryan** *follows suit.*)

Bryan   Oh. Does that mean . . . ?

Lorraine   Yes, of course I'll do it. Would you like a cocktail before you go?

Bryan (*on top of the world*)   But that's wonderful! No, I'd better not, thank you. I'm late as it is. (*He holds out his hand and she shakes it, boyishly.*) I can't tell you how excited I am, and how grateful too.

Lorraine *snatches up the script from the sofa and holds it solemnly.*

Lorraine   This is our talisman. The token of our lovely new friendship.

She kisses him impulsively on the cheek and they look into each other's eyes.

The stage is suddenly filled with activity, and upbeat music breaks in. **Lorraine** *exits. The stage management team of* **Bryan**'s *play,* Dark Heritage, *hurry on and strike the furniture. Exit signs light up and we realise that we are on an empty West End stage. The stage manager,* **Harry Thornton**, *and the assistant stage managers,* **Beryl Fletcher** *and* **Bob Deacon**, *position a long trestle table in the centre of the stage and place chairs around it. A large armchair goes at the head of the table – obviously a tribute to* **Lorraine**'s *star status. On the table are pencils, teacups, plates of biscuits, ashtrays, etc. There is a smaller prompt table on which is a pile of type-written 'parts' bound in dull pink paper.* **Bryan**, *clutching his script, wanders over to a vacant chair, sits down, lights a cigarette and jots down some more notes in his book.*

Scene Three

The music fades. Four cast members have arrived: **Eric Larch**
(good-looking, in his late twenties), **Marion Blake**, **Gerald
Wentworth** *and* **Laura Witby** *(all in their fifties).* **Eric** *is
chatting to* **Laura** *over a coffee;* **Marion** *is sitting at the table
energetically marking up her script with various pens, pencils and a
rubber. She is slightly over-made-up and sports an ostrich feather toque;*
Gerald, *the distinguished leading man, is reading the* Daily
Telegraph.

Ray Malcolm *strides in. The atmosphere, which was already
tense, becomes so charged that one almost expects the stage management
to hand out oxygen masks. Following in* **Ray**'s *slipstream is* **Tony
Orford**, *his assistant and partner.* **Tony**, *who is slightly younger
than* **Ray**, *has a sharp eye and an even sharper tongue. He is wearing
a camel-hair coat and suede shoes.* **Bryan** *gets up eagerly to greet*
Ray, *who ignores him and walks straight over to his stage manager.*
Tony *spots this and grasps* **Bryan**'s *hand.*

Tony   You're Bryan, aren't you? Ray's talked about you
so much that I've been positively counting the minutes. This
is a great day for you. Are you in a terrible tizz?

Bryan   Not at all, I'm just –

Before **Bryan** *can finish his sentence,* **Marion** *leaps in with a shrill
squeal and kisses* **Tony** *effusively.*

Marion   Tony! Ahhh! (*Turning to* **Bryan**.) Hello! I saw
you sitting there and I wasn't sure. But if nobody is going to
introduce us I shall just have to introduce myself. I'm
Marion Blake (or should I say 'Stella'?!) and congratulations
– I just think the play has got everything, but everything!

Bryan   Thank –

Marion   I don't believe I've been so excited about a script
since I first read *Love Child*, and heaven knows I was right
about that.

Tony   *Love Child* was my *un*favourite play of all time.

Marion   Be that as it may, Tony, it ran two solid years and we never dropped, even during the election. (*She turns to* **Bryan**.) Isn't he horrid? He's always doing that to me. So damping.

Ray *raps his pencil on the table. There is a general movement towards the chairs,* **Beryl** *and* **Bob** *distribute the parts and* **Ray** *motions to* **Bryan** *to come and sit next to him.* **Bryan** *does so with a thrill of pride.*

Ray   Is everybody ready to begin? I know that Miss Barrie isn't here yet, but we can start without her as she isn't in the first scene. Firstly I should like to welcome you all, and say how glad I am that we're to work together. For those I haven't met, my name is Ray Malcolm. May I also introduce Tony Orford, my personal assistant, and of course our author, Bryan Snow. (*There is a spatter of applause and* **Bryan** *looks acutely embarrassed.*) Anyone who was lucky enough to catch Mr Snow's previous play, *The Unconquered*, at the Bayswater Theatre Club will know about the raw power of his writing; but in *Dark Heritage* there's no doubt that he really has created something very special.

Gerald *leans across the table to shake hands with* **Bryan**.

Gerald (*in a loud whisper*)   Sorry to interrupt. Wentworth. Gerald Wentworth.

Ray   I am proud to be directing it and I hope for our author, and indeed for all our sakes, that we make a terrific success of it.

Gerald (*amid further applause*)   Hear! hear!

Ray   What I'd like to do this morning is just to have a gentle canter through the play. (**Gerald** *blows his nose.*) I'll dispense with reading the detailed description of the set, because that's awfully boring. Enough to say that (*reading*) 'the whole action of the play takes place in Eleanor Marshall's villa in the south of France. When the curtain rises it is late afternoon. Stella and Aubrey enter. They are

wearing bathrobes over their bathing things.' Thank you,
Marion.

Marion (*Stella*)   I'm absolutely exhausted; that last drag up
the hill –

Gerald   Sorry to stop you, Marion love, but I've been
given this 'part' here. (*He flaps it around.*) I'd just as soon read
from my script if that's all right with you, Ray.

Ray   Yes, of course.

Gerald   Right-ho. Sorry.

Ray   From the beginning again, Marion. Thank you.

Marion (*Stella*)   I'm absolutely exhausted; that last drag up
the hill always seems much longer than I think it's going to
be.

Eric (*Aubrey*)   Where's Eleanor? She's usually home by this
time.

Marion (*Stella*)   She went into Eze to see Roberto.

Ray   'Ez', I think.

Marion   Sorry – Ez. (*Quickly practising the line.*) She went
into Ez to see Roberto. (*Back into character.*) Poor Eleanor, I
can't help feeling sorry for her. She's so – so – vulnerable.
I'm not sure women ought to go on being vulnerable after
forty; it diminishes them.

Eric (*Aubrey*)   To me Eleanor is ageless; I can't imagine her
ever growing old.

At this moment there is a slight commotion in the passage leading to the
stage and the sound of a dog barking. A swing door with 'Silence'
painted on it in large white letters bursts open, and **Lorraine** *comes*
on at a run. She is simply-dressed in a neat blue tailor-made suit and a
small hat. A fur cape hangs from her shoulders and she is hugging to
herself three parcels, a big scarlet handbag, a rolled umbrella, the script
and Bothwell.

Lorraine (*gaily*)   This is quite definitely the worst entrance I've ever made. I know I'm late and I'm bitterly ashamed. Please, please will you all forgive me?

Everyone has stood up, and **Marion**, *emitting shrill noises, rushes across and hugs her emotionally as though she has just been rescued from a foundering liner. In the process,* **Marion**'s *hat gets knocked to one side, giving her a slightly debauched look.*

Marion dear, how lovely to see you. How was your motor trip through Spain? I want to hear all about it at lunch. (*She turns to* **Harry**.) Harry, be an angel and take Bothwell into the property room, and tie him up to something heavy. (*Glancing round for something suitable.*) How about a script of the play? (*Everyone except* **Bryan** *laughs.*) I had to bring him to rehearsal because he was so wretched when he thought I was going to leave him behind. His poor little tail drooped like a weeping willow.

Marion   Will he be all right in the prop room?

Lorraine   Of course. He adores prop rooms, they're a second home to him. (*She hands Bothwell to* **Harry**, *who goes off with him.*) Goodbye, my angel-pie! Ray. (*She deposits her parcels on the table and shakes hands with* **Ray**, *smiling radiantly. Everyone watches.*) Dear Ray Malcolm. Promise you're not angry with me.

Ray   Of course not, Lorraine. We'd only just made a start on the first scene.

Lorraine *sits down at the table and opens her script. Everyone else sits.*

Lorraine (*Smiling graciously to the whole company*)   Good morning, everybody. (*They all smile and say good morning. She spots* **Gerald**.) Gerald darling! In all the excitement I didn't see you there. (**Gerald** *goes across and kisses her hand.* **Lorraine** *looks at him with pained sympathy.*) How's my Hilda?

Gerald   As well as can be expected. Bless you for asking, Lorraine.

Lorraine   My heart aches every time I think of her. (*She rummages for a handkerchief and puts on her horn-rimmed glasses. She leans across the table and pats* **Bryan**'*s hand.*) Good morning, dear author. This is all wildly exciting, isn't it?

Bryan   Yes – yes it is.

Harry *returns.*

Ray   The armchair's for you, Lorraine. Harry rooted it out from somewhere or other specially.

Lorraine (*shaking her head firmly*)   I couldn't, darling, really I couldn't. Once I sank into that I should go into a deep, deep sleep. Marion must have it. (*She beckons to* **Marion**.) Take the comfy chair, Marion.

Marion   No, no, no, no, no! I'm perfectly happy where I am.

Lorraine   Nonsense. I insist.

Marion   Oh. Very well.

Marion *is forced to get up and walk the length of the table with all eyes on her. She sinks down into the deep armchair and is now at least two feet lower than everyone else. Covered with embarrassment, she opens her script.*

Lorraine   Are we starting from the beginning, or from my first entrance?

Ray (*with the merest hint of steel*)   From the beginning.

Lorraine   Lovely, darling – gives me time for a ciggy. (*She picks up her bag again, fumbles in it, finds her cigarette case and takes a cigarette out. About six people lean forward to light it for her, but she waves them away and lights it herself.*)

Ray   All right. Is everybody ready?

There is a general murmur of assent.

Off you go again, Marion.

Marion (*Stella*)   I'm absolutely exhausted; that last drag up the hill always seems much longer than I think it's going to be.

Eric (*Aubrey*)   Where's Eleanor? She's usually home by this time.

Marion (*Stella*)   She went into Eze to see Roberto.

Ray (*patiently*)   Yes, 'Ez', I think.

Marion   So sorry. Ez.

The lights change and music fades in to suggest a time lapse. The lights come back up again and we find that we are now halfway through the play.

Marion (*Stella*)   Was that so very wrong? Why should there be one rule for you and another for me? I love him, Eleanor. It's true: I love him with every fibre of my being.

Lorraine (*Eleanor*)   And does he love you?

Marion (*Stella*)   Yes. He loves me very much. (*She laughs almost hysterically.*) There: I've said it. Of course the fishing trip was mere subterfuge! Don't look at me like that, Ellie. I refuse to feel guilty. (*Skittishly.*) In fact, I feel strangely light-headed!

*During the course of her speech, **Marion** is so carried away that she gets up, script in hand, and stands defiant, acting her heart out. Everyone else looks on, some concealing their horror better than others. The lights change and the music fades in again. When the lights come back up, **Marion** has sat down again and we find that we are now at the end of the play. The company have changed their positions – some have slouched, some are sitting forward intently, several are smoking.*

Gerald (*Mortimer*)   I neither believe nor disbelieve, Stella. With every instinct I have – I know.

Marion (*Stella*)   But she had so much to live for. It all seems so – so futile –

Gerald (*Mortimer*)   It was deliberate.

Marion (*Stella*)   Mortimer don't, don't, don't she sobs uncontrollably – (*She breaks off.*) Whoops – that's a stage direction! What a clot! (*She scribbles in her script, then reads again, all guns blazing.*) Mortimer don't, don't, don't! (*She sobs uncontrollably.*)

Gerald (*Mortimer*)   (*after a good deal of sobbing from* **Marion**) Please, Stella, there's nothing to be gained by continuing this agonising post-mortem. What's done is done. Poor Eleanor was marked for tragedy; I sensed it the first moment I saw her. Her destiny was in her eyes.

Marion (*Stella*)   It was you and I who implemented that destiny; it was we who betrayed her.

Gerald (*Mortimer*)   For God's sake, Stella, be quiet. Do you think I can ever forgive myself for driving her away? We are all responsible for our actions, and we must live with their consequences. Go now; please go. Leave me alone in my shame.

Marion (*Stella*)   You will never be alone again, Mortimer. There will be a ghost haunting your desolate years until the last moment of your life.

Gerald (*Mortimer*)   Go away! Go away! Go away!

Ray   Slow curtain.

There is silence for a moment or two. **Lorraine** *rises, goes over to* **Bryan**, *takes both his hands in hers and kisses him.*

Lorraine (*with touching sincerity*)   You have written a beautiful play, my dear. You should be very proud.

Bryan (*embarrassed but delighted*)   Thank you – thank you very much.

Gerald (*noisily clearing his throat*)   Well done! Well done!

Gerald *claps his hands, and this brings forth a spatter of applause from the others.*

Marion (*dabbing her eyes*)   That last scene! It's unbearable –
quite, quite unbearable. It tears me to shreds – No Acting
Required.

Ray   It's a remarkable piece of writing, and I really don't
think it would be fanciful to describe it as Chekhov *à
l'Anglaise*. Just occasionally I think you'll all have to work to
harness the passion, though. Don't forget that these
characters *are* English, and the more you control the
emotional temperature, the greater the impact on the
audience. For example, Marion – you simply can't play the
whole of Act Three at that pitch –

Lorraine   Darling, it was only the read-through; I think
you've got to allow us a bit of licence on the first day –

Ray (*quelling her with a courteous smile*)   Thank you, Lorraine.
(*She taps her lips chidingly with her right forefinger and starts
rummaging in her bag for her compact.*) So do please, all of you,
remember that Less can sometimes be More. (*Looking at his
watch.*) We'll take an hour's break now. If stage management
could set the furniture, then we can start plotting Act One
straight after lunch. Everybody back at two thirty please.

Bryan   May I just say thank you? I thought you all read
wonderfully.

Everyone smiles and gets up to leave. During the following dialogue,
Harry, **Beryl** *and* **Bob** *move the table and chairs upstage and set
the furniture for the afternoon rehearsal. The dialogue takes place
downstage while the furniture is set.*

Lorraine   Do stop snuffling, Marion, there's a love; your
eyes will be bright red and you'll wear yourself out.

Marion (*smiling through her tears*)   I can't help it, that last
scene really unsettles me.

Lorraine   Well, you've made your point, dear. Now is the
time for all good men and true to buckle their armour and
get on with the job.

Ray   Lorraine, would you give me the pleasure of taking you to lunch?

Lorraine   I'd love that. Harry – be an angel and fetch poor Bothwell. (**Harry** *exits.*) Ray, while we're waiting, I must just have a teeny weeny word.

Lorraine *and* **Ray** *go off into the corner for a pow-wow.*

Tony (*to* **Bryan**, *amid the general packing up*) So, you've been through your baptism of fire. How do you feel?

Bryan   Fine. I thought it went awfully well.

Tony   It'll be splendid. It's a terrific script.

Bryan   Thank you.

Beat.

How long have you been Ray's assistant?

Tony   How charmingly euphemistic. Eleven years, man and boy. (**Bryan** *blushes.*) Where are you going for lunch?

Bryan   I hadn't really thought. I can't say I'm terribly hungry.

Tony   Well, I've brought sandwiches and I've made far too many. Could I unload some on to you?

Bryan   That's very kind, thank you.

Tony *starts to unpack the sandwiches. Meanwhile,* **Harry** *has returned with Bothwell.*

Lorraine (*to Bothwell*)   You've been Mother's sweetheart angel-pie, that's what you've been. A shining example to every other four-footed angel-pie in the profession.

Ray *comes over to* **Bryan** *and* **Tony**. **Lorraine** *gives an over-elaborate demonstration of diplomacy.*

Lorraine   I'll just leave you boys to talk for a moment, while we nip outside for a quick pee-pee.

Lorraine *tiptoes out, clutching Bothwell. Everyone else has now left the stage, and the furniture is in place for the afternoon rehearsal.*

Ray   Bryan, I need to put a thought in your head. It's the ending.

Bryan   What's the matter with it?

Ray   Hearing it read this morning, it didn't quite convince. And I have to say, it is very reminiscent of *The Green Hat.*

Bryan (*defensively*)   I've never read *The Green Hat.*

Ray   It doesn't matter if you've read it or not. Your heroine decides to end it all by crashing a speedboat into a lighthouse at fifty miles an hour. In *The Green Hat*, it's a motor car and an oak tree.

Bryan   It's a little late to start making major alterations now. She's got to commit suicide somehow, hasn't she? It's the climax of the whole play.

Ray   Of course she has. Don't get upset. I've got lots of ideas, masses of suggestions but (*with an eye on his watch*), look, I'd better not go into them now. Just mull it over. (*As he speaks, he reaches across to* **Tony***, takes his cigarette, has a drag and hands it back to him.*) And Marion will have to go. I should never have agreed to that. I don't mind her doing Manchester, but we're not opening in London with her playing Stella. Don't worry, I'll sort it out – I think Carole Wylde's still available.

Bryan   Carol Wylde?!

Ray   Good idea, isn't it?

Lorraine *reappears with Bothwell.* **Ray** *immediately changes tack.*

Ray   Lorraine! Ready for the off? How's old Bothwell?

Lorraine   All done and dusted. Have you had a word with Bryan?

Ray   Yes indeed. Now –

Lorraine (*to* **Bryan**) You don't hate me, do you? I mean, for putting a spanner in the works?

Bryan   Pardon?

Lorraine   I just knew, hearing the scene out loud, that somehow or other she wouldn't do it. I don't know why or how, but it didn't ring true to me. *She* didn't ring true. It was – how can I put it? Contrived! That's the word! Contrived! How you must curse the day I was born! (*To Bothwell.*) Yes, my angel-pie, we really *are* going now, so say goodbye to our brilliant author. (*Waggling Bothwell's paw and doing her Bothwell voice.*) 'Bye, bye, brilliant author.' (*To* **Ray**.) Let's not go to the Ivy, treasure, because everyone we know will be there and they'll twitter at us.

Ray   Whatever you like.

Lorraine   What about Pagioli's?

Ray   Where's that?

Lorraine   Dean Street. Nothing but spaghetti, breadsticks and lethal Chianti, but at least it's quiet. You mentioned *The Green Hat*, didn't you?

Ray   Yes.

Lorraine   Good. (*To* **Bryan**.) Only we musn't be seen to be pinching ideas. The critics will be on to it in a flash. (*To* **Ray**.) Come along. (*She blows a quick kiss to* **Bryan**.)

Ray *squeezes* **Bryan***'s arm and leaves with* **Lorraine**.

Bryan (*turning to* **Tony** *in disbelief*) That's outrageous. I don't know anything about the wretched *Green Hat*. Besides, I did write this play, and I know what the characters in it would do and what they wouldn't do because I created them. Nobody else did – I did. Everyone read the play and approved it, otherwise I wouldn't be standing here now, and yet suddenly they decide after the first read-through that no, actually they don't like it after all.

Tony   Balls! They love it – and so they bloody well should.
Come and have a coffee.

During the following dialogue, **Tony** *unscrews his thermos flask and
pours out two cups. Then he sits on a table and starts to munch the
sandwiches, offering them to* **Bryan** *at the same time.*

And believe me, they wouldn't be wasting their time on it if
they didn't feel it had an excellent chance of success.
Unfortunately, the fact is that although Ray has genius as a
director, he's really a frustrated writer. He would give his
eyeteeth to write one page of creative dialogue, but he can't
– and what's more he knows he can't, because writing is a
gift. Either you have it, or you don't. But when Lorraine got
at him just now about the end of the play, that gave him an
excuse to jump in with both feet. (*Indicating the sandwiches.*)
Go on, dig in.

Bryan   Thanks.

Tony   Just remember that it's your play and nobody else's.

Bryan *smiles uneasily.*

Tony   Do you have a . . . personal assistant, Bryan?

Bryan *looks at him. He has begun to warm to* **Tony**, *but is unsure
quite what the question implies. He hesitates.*

Bryan   This is only my second play – what would I do
with one?

Beat.

What was Ray saying about Marion? He mustn't sack her.
With a bit of rehearsal she'll be all right, won't she?

Tony   Sweet God, Bryan, she's *terrible*!

Bryan   Just rather nervous, I expect.

Tony   No. I'll be honest with you: before today I thought
I'd give her the benefit of the doubt. But I'm sorry – after
this morning's death-dealing display, after that vomit-
making welter of gurgles and cooings, that soul-destroying

archness, that hideous, protracted agony of boredom, now, *now* – oh, baby! – I'm glad she's going to get the chop. Glad, glad, glad! And, what's more, I hope she suffers and remains out of work and in dire poverty for seventeen and a half years.

Bryan (*abashed*)   Right. I tell you who won't be quite so pleased though, and that's Lorraine.

Tony   I'll say. Luckily Ray has the right to fire anyone he likes. But even so, I can't wait to see how Madam chooses to retaliate. I should think she's capable of inflicting torture that would make the Marquis de Sade sob with envy.

Bryan   Oh dear. What do you think she'll do?

Tony   Not possessing the gift of clairvoyance, I am unable to tell you what she will do or how and when she will do it. But I'd certainly suggest that you tighten your safety belt and prepare for a crash landing.

Bryan *stares ahead desolately, but* **Tony**'*s enjoying himself no end.*

Tony   Talking of *La Belle Lorraine,* I wonder how she's getting on.

Bryan   Mmm?

Tony   I saw a glint in the Maestro's eye. He generally waits a day or two until he's sure of his ground, but I suspect he's going to start work on her right away.

Bryan   What do you mean, 'start work on her'?

Tony   Oh, he'll be using his little lunch to draw up the battle lines.

He jumps up and moves the prompt table centre stage, placing a chair on either side.

First of all he'll get her with her back to the wall on a red plush banquette. Then, when they've downed the inevitable spaghetti and they're lingering over a coffee, when the atmosphere is cosy, informal and nauseatingly friendly, he will proceed methodically to tear the liver and lights out of her.

He places two coffee cups on the table as **Lorraine** *and* **Ray** *enter and sit down as if at the Italian restaurant. The lighting suggests an intimate Soho bistro.*

Bryan (*getting up and coming across, sandwich in hand*)   That's awful. She didn't mean to be unkind just now.

Tony   Oh no, it's nothing to do with that.

Bryan   Then what's the matter? She read well enough for a first go.

Tony   Oh, you poor innocent dreamer, I don't know whether to slap you or kiss you.

Bryan   Please don't do either until I've finished my sandwich.

Tony *pours out some coffee from his thermos into the two cups; a Neapolitan folk song plays faintly in the background.*

Lorraine (*mid-conversation*)   Can you smell that coffee? Mmmmm. Heaven with the gate shut. (*To* **Tony**/*waiter.*) *Grazie mille, mio caro.* (*Back to* **Ray**.) D'you know, I always leave here feeling wanted and needed and just a teeny bit pampered.

Tony *and* **Bryan** *retire to the shadows and watch.*

Lorraine   Simple peasant fare it may be, but how preferable that is to fussy food and foolish folk. Never, until the grave closes over me, will I go to the Caprice again. I was there last night, and, my dear, the world and his boyfriend were there. The strain was too much. I left utterly worn out.

Ray (*picking up her tone*)   I must say I only eat out these days when I really have to. I'm so much happier stopping home with a good book and a little something on a tray.

Lorraine   I have a sneaking suspicion, Ray, that we are going to be soulmates, you and I. I have a very good feeling for these things. And d'you know, I'm sitting here, rather pleased with myself, rather smug, because – clever old me – I've found myself a play that I adore, a very *sympathique* leading man (isn't he a lamb?) and a director who is not only brilliantly talented but extremely charming to boot. So I would say, correct me if I'm wrong, that God's in his heaven and all's tickety-boo with the world.

Ray   I'm sorry, Lorraine, but I don't think I can allow you a monopoly on good fortune. I'm doing quite nicely too, I'll have you know. You see, I was listening to you earlier, and the way you homed in on the weaknesses in our final scene – back in the rehearsal room, I mean –

Lorraine (*earnestly*)   Yes, my love?

Ray   Well, that reminded me (God! As if I needed reminding!) that you really do possess the most uncanny actor's instinct.

Lorraine (*apparently needing clarification*)   Really? Oh, I just –

Ray   No, Lorraine, you don't need me to tell you that. The simple fact is that you know what you're talking about. And I was thinking not only that I'm lucky enough to be directing you, but that I'd sooner have your thoughts on a new play than almost anyone else I know.

Lorraine   I've been around a long time.

Ray   Yes, but it's more than that. Intellectual acumen is all well and good, but when it's allied to split-second timing, to a quite extraordinary physicality, to a gift for expressing, *without apparent effort*, the subtle nuances of either comedy or tragedy, then one's talking about something, well, something unique. I'm not saying I've always felt that your material was worthy of your talent. I'd be lying if I did, and we don't need to lie to one another. But you are talking to a man who saw *The Cup That Cheers* –

Lorraine (*doing the sign of the cross, and having the time of her life*) Did you have to spoil my lunch?!

Ray   But even in that, you managed to endow a – frankly – turgid, dishonest play with a heart-stopping, luminous truth.

Lorraine   Jimmy was very clever with that, of course.

Ray (*pausing for thought*)   In a way, haven't you hit on something there?

Lorraine   Beg pardon?

Ray   Well, you see, my contention is that you haven't always been best served by your directors. Yes, Jimmy *was* marvellous, Jimmy was *absolutely* marvellous, but how long ago did he pass away?

Lorraine (*wiping away a tear*)   Poor darling.

Ray   Since then . . . well, I'm just trying to think what you've done. There was the thing Scott Gurney directed, but with the best will in the world –

Lorraine   No, darling, you're quite right. It was a mouldy script from the word go, but with that red-faced, drunken little butcher in charge we didn't stand a chance. No, it's true, I have felt bereft.

Ray (*after a pause; significantly*)   That's very interesting.

Lorraine   Yes?

Ray   I just always think that people become trickier when they're unhappy.

Lorraine   I'm sorry?

Ray   Well . . . no, maybe you'd rather not discuss it. But I do think – and yes, we can be honest with each other – I just do think it's a shame that your reputation has been tarnished in the last few years, at least within the profession, by one or two unfortunate stories. I'm talking now about gossip of course, and who's to believe what people say anyway. But I was, I'll confess it, (*choosing the word carefully*) saddened by your late arrival at rehearsal today.

Lorraine (*stunned by the turn in the conversation*)   I thought I'd explained about –

Ray   Sorry, can I just finish? You see, what happened there showed a lack of respect not just to me – and obviously that's not a problem – but also to the company, and particularly to Bryan Snow, whose first commercial play this is. I think we've got to be a wee bit careful about these things.

Lorraine   I –

Ray (*lightly dismissing her protests*)   No, I don't want to dwell on all that. Let's talk about the play, which is much more important. Let's have a look at the central role. Eleanor. This is a part that's going to take you into a new area, an area that I think could be very exciting for you and for your audience. Having said that, there's one thing that concerns me a little. What you were giving me in the read-through was extremely deft, all very expert, but you were allowing one or two mannerisms – little technical tricks, everyone has them – to obscure the essential truth of the writing. There's a wonderful core of simplicity to Bryan's work, and what I was getting from you this morning – and from some of the others too, to a lesser extent – was a finesse, a theatrical polish, a coyness here, an archness there, that is completely and utterly out of place.

There is a long pause. **Ray** *sips his coffee and takes out his wallet. He puts a couple of banknotes on the table.*

Now, the only reason I've said all this is that I sincerely believe you to be a great, great actress. And I am determined that your performance as Eleanor Marshall will be the finest achievement of what is, by any standards, a dazzling career.

Lorraine   . . . Thank you, Ray.

Ray   I also know that you're a professional, and that, like me, you want to get it right. You get satisfaction not from the blandishments of Fleet Street hacks, but from a job well done.

Pause. **Ray** *looks at his watch.*

We'd better get back, or you'll be accusing *me* of bad time-keeping!

They both stand, **Lorraine** *a bit unsteadily.* **Ray** *goes round and helps her up, kissing her tenderly on the cheek.* **Tony**, *in waiter mode, helps her on with her cape which she'd placed over the back of her chair.* **Lorraine** *takes* **Ray**'s *arm and they leave the stage. The lights come up.*

Tony (*pocketing* **Ray**'s *money*)   And off they'll go, arm-in-arm, just as they came in – but with one major difference. Lorraine's inner security will have been shattered. She'll be fussed and bewildered and considerably more pliable. The results will be discernible on a clear day during the second week of rehearsal.

Bryan   But why does he need to assert himself over her? Why take it for granted that she's going to be tiresome? It's all so cynical. You'd drop dead from shock, wouldn't you, if we got through this whole production without a single argument.

Tony   I certainly would, but before I breathed my last, I'd take the trouble to write you a cheque for a thousand pounds.

Bryan   Is that a bet?

Tony   No. But it's a promise.

Suddenly the swing door opens and **Ray** *comes in, followed by* **Marion**, **Gerald**, **Eric**, **Laura** *and the stage management team – all back from lunch. He walks straight over to* **Tony** *and* **Bryan** *while everyone prepares to start the afternoon rehearsal.*

Ray   Go and see to Lorraine, would you, Tony, she's a bit down in the dumps. I think she's powdering her nose. Tell her I won't need her for at least half an hour.

Tony (*on his way out*)   'I go, I go, look how I go! Swifter than an arrow from Raymond's bow . . .'

Bryan   Would this be a good moment to have a word about the rewrite?

Ray   No. I need to get on with the rehearsal. It's probably best if you cut along now, Bryan.

Bryan   Oh, I was hoping to stay.

Ray   No, the actors get jumpy if the writer's always in the room. Don't worry about the ending. I won't touch Act Three until next week – that'll give us some breathing space. But I'd like you to come down to the cottage at the weekend, and we can hash it all over then. Yes?

Bryan (*elated*)   Thank you, Ray. I'd love that.

Ray (*shaking his hand*)   Good. Small suitcase, no dinner clothes, just ourselves.

Bryan   That'll be wonderful.

Ray   You know, Bryan (**Bryan** *turns back to him, and* **Ray** *fixes him with the full force of his concentrated charm*), working with you is a real delight.

Ray *smiles and* **Bryan** *drifts out, unable to think of anything coherent to say.*

Right, are we all ready? We'll start from the beginning. Marion and Eric, if you could enter stage right, through the door here.

Marion (*indicating a vast, tatty dressing gown that she's wearing*) I found this on a rail and thought it might do, just for now, as my bathrobe. What do you think?

Ray   Fine.

Marion   Or does it just look silly?

Ray   I won't lie to you, Marion, it looks absurd, but I'm really not too bothered about that at the moment. Just go over there with Eric.

Marion   Right. Sorry to be a nuisance. (*Holding up a scarf.*) And can we pretend that this is a towel?

Ray   We can try.

Marion   Make a start then, shall we?

Ray (*with extreme politeness*)   If you'd be so kind.

Marion (*Stella*)   (*drying her hair with the scarf*) I'm absolutely exhausted; that last drag up the hill always seems much longer than I think it's going to be.

Eric (*Aubrey*)   Where's Eleanor? She usually home by this time.

Marion (*Stella*)   She went into . . . Ez to see Roberto! (*She looks triumphantly at the assembled crowd, who burst into spontaneous applause –* **Ray** *excepted.*)

Blackout. Music breaks in.

Scene Four

As the lights come up, we see that we are now in the guest bedroom of **Ray** *and* **Tony**'s *cottage in Kent. The furniture laid out for the rehearsal in the previous scene provides the setting: a single bed, a bedside table and lamp, a doorway and a small desk with an upright chair.* **Bryan**, *clad in striped pyjamas, is sitting up in bed, writing in his notebook. His various drafts of* Dark Heritage *are strewn all over the desk, next to his typewriter.*

As the music fades, a cock crows and **Tony** *comes into the room, bearing* **Bryan**'s *early morning tea on a tray. He's wearing a peacock-blue and scarlet sarong and is naked from the waist up.*

Tony   It's all right, dear. It's only me and not Dorothy Lamour as you thought. (*Placing the tray down on the bedside table, and pouring out a cup.*) My sister sends me these things from Malaya. They're wonderful to sleep in, and you can kick your legs about all night long if you feel like it without strangling yourself. (*Sitting down on the bed.*) Now – sweet dreams?

Bryan   No, I'm afraid I couldn't sleep. (*He throws down his notebook.*) Oh, I wish I'd never tried to write this blasted play in the first place. Ray's set on a new draft of Act Three and, for all his suggestions, I haven't the foggiest where to begin.

Tony   In which case, stop worrying and drink your tea. I am your fairy godmother and all I have to do is wave my magic wand, which, alas, until this morning I was unable to locate owing to the cold weather.

Bryan *manages a forced smile and sips his tea.* **Tony** *lights a cigarette.*

Tony   If this sends you off into a frenzy of vomiting I'll put it out.

Bryan (*betraying his slight irritation*)   I didn't even know you were here.

Tony   I came down last night on the late train. I love my weekends in the country, and anyway I thought I should be on hand in case Herr Direktor takes it into his head to rewrite the entire play.

Bryan   Oh dear.

Tony   Don't tell me! I bet he never drew breath all the way down in the car, came up with fifteen different endings – all ghastly – and now the whole of Act Three looks like a dog's dinner.

Bryan   It does rather.

Tony   And I suppose he played out every scene and tore himself to shreds?

Bryan   I think I was the one who was torn to shreds.

Tony (*patting **Bryan**'s foot affectionately*)   You poor dear.
This happens with every new play he directs. Don't think
I'm being disloyal to the infant Reinhardt – I adore him and
admire him more than anybody in the world. But I do know
his failings, and his principal one is that he can't let well
alone. What's important, of course, is whether the end of
the play is right as it is, or whether it *should* be altered. So
come on then: cards on the table, shoulders to the wheel,
wigs on the green – what do you think yourself? Really and
honestly.

Bryan   I don't know. I feel a bit muddled. Assuming that I
can't have the crash because, *apparently*, it's stolen from a
novel I've never even read, what other sorts of suicide are
there? She can't jump under the Blue Train – Tolstoy's
already bagged that one.

Tony   She can't shoot herself offstage.

Bryan   Why not? Oh yes, Mrs Tanqueray.

Tony   And Pinero pinched that from Chekhov.

Bryan   Who filched it from Ibsen. Sleeping tablets would
take too long, and we'd have to stick in a time lapse.

Tony   It's a shame really there are no ramparts to fall
from. And somehow I can't see Lorraine Barrie impaling
herself on a samurai sword (much as we'd all love her to).
But could I make one small, insignificant suggestion?

Bryan (*wary*)   Of course. I'd be very grateful.

Tony   Let her live.

Bryan   What?

Tony   Allow the audience to think that she really is going
to do herself in. Then have her pull herself together, and, at
the end, after the cocktail scene, get all the others out on to
the terrace, and let the curtain fall on her telephoning
Mortimer, quietly and bravely, with a smile on her lips and

tears rolling down her cheeks. It's not so obviously dramatic as the way you've written it . . . (*as if the idea's just struck him*) but I think it could be more real.

There's a long pause during which **Tony** *offers* **Bryan** *a cigarette and lights it for him.* **Tony** *attempts to blow a smoke ring or two.*

Bryan (*thinking it through*)   It'd mean a pretty substantial rewrite, but . . . yes . . . Actually I can see it working quite well.

Tony   Think it over quietly, and don't allow yourself to be bullied. More tea?

Bryan (*holding out his cup*)   Thanks.

Tony   And if I were you, I wouldn't say a word about it to the Maestro until you've got it down on paper.

Bryan   No, right. I think perhaps I'll try and type up the key points now.

Tony   Why not?

Bryan *gets out of bed, throws on a dressing gown and goes over to the desk.*

Bryan (*suddenly troubled*)   What happens if Lorraine still doesn't like it?

Tony   Then I have a very neat suggestion as to what she can do with it.

They can't help giggling, and **Tony** *lobs a pillow at* **Bryan**, *who chucks it back at him just as* **Ray** *appears in the doorway. He's wearing a dressing gown, and has the Sunday paper under his arm. He's rattled by the sight of the other two.*

Ray   So this is where the party is. Are you ever coming down, or are you just going to let Mrs Hartley's breakfast congeal on the plate?

Tony   There's no need to sound quite so pious. A quarter of an hour ago you were stretched out like a fish on a slab.

Bryan   I'm awfully sorry, Ray. We've been discussing the play.

Ray (*almost jealous*)   Have you?

Tony   Yes, and Bryan's solved all the problems.

Bryan   I don't know about that. I –

Ray   Then you'd better come down and tell me all about it.

Bryan   Would you mind terribly if I stayed up here for a bit, Ray? I'm not really hungry, and I would love to make some notes while everything's fresh in my mind.

Ray   If you must. What's the big idea then?

Bryan   I hope you'll like it. It's better than the old version at any rate. (*To* **Tony**.) Do you know, I'm almost embarrassed to think how melodramatic it was, I –

Ray   Yes, it certainly needed a complete rethink. So?

Beat.

I'm waiting.

Bryan (*reluctant to go into details*)   Well . . .

Tony (*to* **Ray**)   I thought you were the one who wanted breakfast. Come on, let's leave the Boy Wonder to work his alchemy in peace.

Ray (*ignoring* **Tony**)   How long will it take you to cobble it together?

Bryan (*feeling a stab of panic*)   I don't know. Probably not more than a day or two.

Ray   Good God! As long as that. Well, you better stay here until it's finished. We've got to go back to town tonight –

Tony   Have we? Why?

Ray   Drinks party at Binkie's.

Tony   God help us.

Ray   But you can sit tight. Mrs Hartley will be here to wait on you hand and foot.

Bryan   That's very kind.

Tony   And she'll report back to the Commandant if she catches you slacking.

Ray   I'm afraid I'm serious. Rehearsals are going to be scuppered if I don't have the new draft within forty-eight hours. There are a number of reputations riding on this play, Bryan, yours included. We'll be downstairs.

He leaves the room. Silence.

Tony   Have you finished with the tea?

Bryan   Yes.

Tony *picks up the tray, balancing it on the upturned palm of his hand like a waiter.*

Bryan   I can't tell you how grateful I am, Tony. I wonder if I could talk the scene through with you again later – if you can spare the time.

Tony   All the time in the world.

Bryan   Thank you very much.

Tony   That's all right.

He lowers the tray and wanders across to **Bryan**, *looking at him quizzically.*

I suppose my reward will just have to be in heaven . . .

We hear **Ray**'s *voice, calling from downstairs.*

Ray (*fiercely*)   Tony!!

Tony (*rolling his eyes*)   'His Master's Voice'.

He saunters out, closing the door behind him. **Bryan** *is utterly dejected. He slumps down in front of his typewriter and distractedly* *tidies up his papers. Then he looks at his watch. Music creeps in. The lights slowly fade, apart from the warm summer sun which floods in through the window on to the desk.* **Bryan** *starts to type. As his writing picks up momentum, the music swells, and suddenly he's forgotten all about* **Ray** *and* **Tony** *and is completely absorbed. He taps away frantically and we have a —*

Blackout.

Act Two

Scene One

The curtain is in. We hear a rather scratchy panatrope recording of music from Ivor Novello's Glamorous Night. *The music fades, the tab warmers slowly go down and the curtain flies out to reveal a meticulously traditional stage set. It should resemble a still from* Play Pictorial *c. 1951, taking us back to a West End world before the arrival of John Osborne. It represents the terrace of Eleanor Marshall's villa on the Cap d'Antibes.*

We are watching the technical dress rehearsal of Dark Heritage. **Lorraine** *and* **Gerald** *are on stage, dressed as Eleanor and Mortimer, but, despite the old-fashioned setting, they are acting so well that it doesn't feel like acting.*

Lorraine (*Eleanor*)   Why did you come? What do you think can be gained by this?

Gerald (*Mortimer*)   I came here because I had to, it's as simple as that. If it hadn't been for this afternoon, I might have had the strength to stay away, but catching sight of you like that in the street was more than I could bear. I suddenly felt so lonely, as if I were of no more importance to you than the other passers-by.

Lorraine (*Eleanor*)   You *are* of no more importance than them.

Gerald (*Mortimer*)   I know I asked for that, but I still don't believe it.

Lorraine (*Eleanor*)   Please go. This weak, flabby sentimentality is not only unworthy of you, but of everything we have been to each other. For God's sake have the courage of your own convictions.

Gerald (*Mortimer*)   I had convictions once – erm (*searching for the words*), er – I had convictions once, or at least I thought I had, but not any more.

Lorraine (*Eleanor*)   Beware of self-pity, it's a dangerous indulgence.

Gerald (*Mortimer*)   I deluded myself that I had the guts to make a clean break, but I was wrong, I hadn't – I – I – I was wrong, I hadn't – I –

There's an awkward pause. Suddenly we hear **Ray***'s voice calling from the back of the stalls.*

Ray   Do you want to go back and work into it, Gerald?

Gerald   No thanks, love. I'm better if I keep going.

He looks out front, shielding his eyes from the glare of the lights.

Awfully sorry, everybody. I knew it backwards in the bath this morning.

Lorraine   Perhaps if you had a scrub now it might come back to you. I'm sure we don't mind waiting. We could all pop over to the Dog and Fox and have a nice ham sandwich.

Gerald   It's just this scene. I've got a mental block about it. (*Back into character.*) I deceived myself –

Lorraine   'Deluded myself'.

Gerald   Sorry. Deluded. Thanks.

Lorraine (*acidly*)   Don't mention it.

Gerald (*Mortimer*)   I deluded myself that I had the guts to make a clean break, but I was wrong, I hadn't.

Beat.

Lorraine   'Please, Eleanor'.

Gerald (*Mortimer*)   Please, Eleanor, don't harden your heart quite yet. Not quite yet. You don't suppose it was easy, do you, for me to come to you, cap in hand like this, abjectly begging to be given just one more chance to prove –

Lorraine (*Eleanor*)   To prove what?

Gerald (*Mortimer*)   That I love you. In spite of everything, and because of everything, I love you. I shall never love anyone else, ever in my life!

He takes her in his arms. She struggles for a moment and then submits.

Lorraine (*Eleanor*)   Mortimer!

Her belt falls off and she immediately comes out of character.

God damn it! I knew that would happen. (*She marches down to the footlights.*) I'm sorry, Ray, but this dress is driving me mad. It looks like I'm wearing a deck chair.

Ray   All right, I'm coming down. (*He walks down the aisle and up on to the stage, followed by* **Tony**, *who is clutching a notebook.*)

Lorraine   I said I needed another fitting before we left London. Nora?

Nora (*from the wings*)   Coming!

People trickle on to the stage from all directions to take advantage of the hiatus. **Eric** *practises opening and shutting the French windows;* **Harry** *comes across to* **Gerald** *and shows him the prompt copy of the script, so he can check his lines;* **Beryl** *polishes the table;* **Bob** *attaches some trailing ivy to the wall;* **Laura**, *in maid's uniform, rehearses loading and unloading a tray of cocktails;* **Nora**, *with a mouthful of pins, attends to* **Lorraine**'s *dress.*

Lorraine   I'd give my immortal soul for a cup of coffee.

Marion, *dressed as Stella, calls out from the stalls.*

Marion   I'll get one for you, Lorry! Don't worry, I've got some change on me . . . ! (*She hurries up on to the stage and off through the wings.*)

Ray *consults* **Tony**'s *notebook.*

Ray   While we've stopped, Harry, could you strike that lemon tree – it masks the whole corner of the stage, and, er

. . . (*checking his notes*) oh yes, this table's too far up. Move it downstage a foot and change the marks. (**Harry** *proceeds to do so.*)

Lorraine   Couldn't we change the chair too while we're at it? It's hell to play on. It feels more like a hip bath.

Tony   It looks fine from the front, Lorraine.

Lorraine   Yes, well it's not easy being witty and fascinating with your knees hitting your chin, that's all I'm saying. (*To* **Gerald**.) Sit in it, darling, and you'll see what I mean.

Gerald *sinks into the chair and bounces up and down a bit.*

Gerald   It certainly is a bit low.

Lorraine   A bit low?! You're practically on the floor; we'll need a crane to hoist you out. Give me a cigarette, somebody, I'm gasping.

Tony (*proferring his case*)   Madam!

Lorraine (*shuddering*)   No, darling, those flat Turkish sausages are far too grand for me. Hasn't anyone got a Players?

Eric   Here, Lorry.

Eric *produces a packet of Players.* **Lorraine** *takes one and he lights it for her. It's an intimate moment.*

Lorraine (*very much in love*)   Thanks.

Meanwhile, **Ray** *has been in the wings, and now returns.*

Ray   I thought so. That cloth needs stretching, Harry. I can't be doing with a wrinkly sky.

Tony   Especially on the Côte d'Azur.

Ray   Marion? (*He grabs* **Tony***'s notebook.*) Where's Marion?

Lorraine (*sitting on the* chaise longue)   She's just popped out to fetch me a cup of coffee.

Ray   Typical.

Lorraine   She won't be a minute; she gets it from the Kardomah.

Ray   I don't care if she gets it from Venezuela, the fact remains that she isn't here and she should be. I expect every member of the cast to stand by during a dress rehearsal.

Lorraine   Well, on this occasion it's my fault.

Ray   No, it isn't. You merely encourage her. Marion has a mania for running errands for other people. In a previous life she must have been a carrier pigeon.

Lorraine   You really mustn't be beastly about Marion. She's devoted to you.

Ray   That implies no particular distinction. Marion is devoted to everyone. Where's Eric?

Eric *is lying on the floor, caressing* **Lorraine***'s feet.*

Eric   Here here.

Ray   What's that line you have in the first scene about Eleanor? Something about her recklessness.

Eric   Erm, 'There's something inherently reckless in Eleanor's character.'

Ray   Yes. I think it should be 'in*her*ently' – not 'inherently'.

Eric   Right. It's just 'in*her*ently' sounds a bit odd to me. After all, one doesn't say 'in*her*itance'.

Ray   Good point. Author!

Bryan (*calling out from the stalls*)   Change it to 'innately'. (*He walks down to the front of the auditorium.*)

Ray (*smiling at him*)   That's cheating. Check it. (*To* **Eric**.) Say 'innately' for the time being.

Gerald *has been lying back in the armchair with his eyes closed. Now he chips in.*

Gerald   While we're on the subject of lines being tricky to say, could I venture a tiny cut in that scene with Lorraine?

Ray   What is it?

Gerald   It's when I say (*deliberately making a meal of the speech*) 'You don't suppose it was easy – do you – for me – to come to you – cap in hand – like this – abjectly begging to be given just one more chance etc. etc. etc.'. I'd dearly love to cut 'cap in hand'. It doesn't half hold up the sentence. Also I haven't got a cap.

Bryan   You don't have to have one. It's not supposed to be literal – it's a figure of speech.

Lorraine   I must say I do see what Gerald means. I always want to laugh when he says it. It somehow makes a funny picture. I see him in a flat cap. 'Eee by gum!' (*Everyone laughs.*)

Eric   'Ay up – trouble at Mill!'

Gerald   'Well, I'll go to the foot of our stairs!' (*Apart from* **Bryan***, they all find this hilarious.*)

Bryan (*suppressing his irritation*)   Cut it by all means, if you want to.

Gerald   Thanks, love. I think that's why I've been finding the scene such a pig to learn. You get a superfluous phrase like that and your whole rhythm goes.

Ray   If you've all finished nibbling at poor Bryan's play, we'll press on. We'd better pick up from where your dress disintegrated, Lorraine. Just give me time to get back to my seat.

Ray *and* **Tony** *return to the stalls, and everyone leaves the stage apart from* **Lorraine** *and* **Gerald***, who prepare to start again.*

Lorraine   Do you think, darling, that when you take me in your arms you could be a tiny bit less emotional? I think that's what snapped my belt.

Gerald   How do you mean?

Lorraine   Just walk it a minute and I'll show you. (*To the stalls.*) Won't be a moment. (*Prompting him.*) 'That I love you . . .'

Gerald (*without expression*)   That I love you. In spite of everything, and because of everything, I love you. I shall never love anyone else, ever in my life.

Lorraine   Mortimer. (*He takes her in his arms.*) There now, you've done it again.

Gerald   Done what again? Broken the belt?

Lorraine   No, the belt's all right. But you nearly winded me. It's something to do with your elbow. It sort of digs into me.

Gerald   You never said anything about it before.

Lorraine   You've never done it before. You're probably a bit on edge because it's the dress rehearsal. We all are.

Gerald   I'm not in the least on edge. I just don't know what you're fussing about.

Lorraine   I'm not 'fussing', Gerald. I'm merely asking you to be careful. This is supposed to be a love scene, not an all-in wrestling match.

Gerald   I'm sure I'll get there in the end, Lorraine. Just give me time.

Lorraine   I've given you three weeks. This scene is the keynote of the play and unless we play it smoothly and accurately, we're sunk.

Gerald   I quite agree. (*With an edge in his voice.*) But I doubt if we can achieve either smoothness or accuracy if we're going to lose our temper over trivialities.

Lorraine   I have not lost my temper, but I most certainly will if you speak to me in that tone.

Gerald   If you don't like working with me, you don't have to. I shall be in my dressing room.

Gerald *stalks off the stage and into the wings. There is dead silence for a moment.* **Lorraine** *realises that everybody has been watching. She walks down to the footlights.*

Lorraine   I'm sorry, Ray, deeply sorry. That was all my fault.

Ray (*from the stalls*)   I'm coming up.

There is a further silence as **Ray** *and* **Tony** *walk down the aisle and up on to the stage.* **Lorraine** *bites her lip and goes up to the French windows, ostensibly to control her nerves, but actually to work up a few tears.* **Ray** *and* **Tony** *go into conference, sotto voce, at the front of the stage.*

Ray   It'll be murder from now on. She's just revving up, and she won't be satisfied until the whole company's in a state of jitters.

Tony   Don't let her get the better of you. Take the offensive. You know you're stronger than she is.

Ray   Yes. Of course I am. You go and sort out Gerald.

Lorraine (*throwing herself on his mercy*)   Please forgive me, Ray.

Ray   Yes, yes, yes.

Tony *hurries off into the wings.*

Lorraine   I've been on hot coals ever since I set foot in Manchester. And just look at me: the wig's a disaster, this frock *isn't* right and now, to crown it all, Gerald Wentworth hates me. I'm sure you think I'm a perfect beast, but I'm not, really I'm not, it's just – (*Her voice breaks.*) It's just that suddenly everything seems to be too much for me. (*She sinks into the armchair.*)

Ray   Snap out of it, there's a good girl. You seemed happy with the frock at the dress parade yesterday.

Lorraine (*through her tears*)   I wasn't called upon to play a love scene at the dress parade yesterday. I merely put the damned thing on and took it off again.

Tony (*appearing from the wings*)   Harry's trying to coax Gerald out of his dressing room.

Lorraine (*wiping her eyes*)   What are we going to do about him, Ray? He barely knows a syllable of it. And why was he off in the first act? How do you miss an entrance like that?

Ray (*turning to* **Tony**)   Yes, how did that happen?

Tony   *I* don't know. Perhaps we should employ a guide dog to nuzzle him on to the stage. We could always train up Bothwell.

Lorraine   It's all very fine for you to make jokes, Tony. You don't have to play love scenes with the clumsy great ox.

Tony   He'd be mighty surprised if I did.

Lorraine   Nobody else would. (*They all three laugh.*)

At this moment, **Marion** *returns with the refreshments, holding the cup away from her dress. She's wearing a coat over her shoulders.*

Marion   Coffee up! (*Seeing* **Ray** *and* **Tony** *sharing a joke with* **Lorraine**.) Oh, lovely, are we having a break? (*She hands the coffee to* **Lorraine**.)

Ray   Actually that's quite a good idea. (*Calling into the wings.*) Take a ten-minute break, everyone. (*To the stalls.*) Ten minutes. (*To* **Tony**.) Come on, let's get a coffee. Will you be all right, Lorraine?

Lorraine   Yes, fine, darling, bless you.

Ray *and* **Tony** *head off into the wings. The stage is empty, apart from* **Lorraine** *and* **Marion**.

Lorraine (*leaning right back and relaxing*)   D'you know I'm whacked.

Marion (*sitting on an upright chair*)   I'm glad they've gone.
I've . . . I've got something to tell you.

Lorraine   I shouldn't be drinking this in costume, you
know. And on the set too. Breaking all the rules! So. What's
the matter?

Marion   I don't know that anything's the matter really.
I'm . . . I'm just a bit worried.

Lorraine   You're being very mysterious. What's
happened?

Marion   Who do you think I saw walking past the theatre
just now?

Lorraine   For heaven's sake, Marion, stop being so
cryptic. Who did you see?

Marion   Carole Wylde.

Lorraine (*sitting up with a start*)   Carole Wylde?!

Marion   I just thought it was such a coincidence that *she*
should be in Manchester too. And she was carrying a script
under her arm.

Lorraine (*calling into the stalls*)   Nora?! (*She tries to get up, but
the chair is so deep that she can't. Calling into the wings.*) Nora!!

Nora (*from the wings*)   Yes, dear?

Lorraine   Come here. (*To* **Marion**.) Help me up!

Marion *puts down the coffees and yanks* **Lorraine** *up.* **Nora**
appears, clutching a newspaper.

Lorraine   Run to the Kardomah and find Mr Malcolm.
Tell him I wish to see him urgently in my dressing room.

Nora   Right you are. (*She goes.*)

Lorraine (*with mounting fury*)   How could he? How *could*
he?!

Marion   I don't want to upset you, darling, by burdening you with my troubles at a moment like this –

Lorraine   Don't say another word, Marion.

Marion   You've always been such a wonderful friend to me, Lorry, such a wonderful friend –

Lorraine (*pointing to the wings*)   Go to your dressing room, Marion, and don't come out of it until I send for you.

Marion   I knew Ray hated me – I've felt it all through rehearsals. If it hadn't been for you, and all your sweetness to me, I couldn't have borne it, I know I couldn't.

Lorraine   Never mind about that now.

Marion *goes to speak.*

Lorraine   Marion! Not another word!

Music breaks in. **Marion** *exits;* **Lorraine** *takes off her dress and puts on a man's dressing gown. As the walls of the set fly out, the lighting changes to suggest that we are now in* **Lorraine**'s *dressing room (again suggested simply by the furniture).*

Scene Two

Lorraine *sits in front of her mirror in her dressing gown and dark glasses, with an expression of grim determination. The music stops. There is a knock at the door.*

Lorraine   Come in.

Ray *and* **Bryan** *enter.*

Ray   You sent for me?

Lorraine   No, Ray, I did not *send* for you. I merely told Nora to ask if you would be kind enough to come and see me for a moment.

Ray   Well, here I am.

Lorraine   Yes. (*She indicates the sofa with a weary gesture. The two men sit down.*) I didn't expect a deputation.

Ray   I presume that what you want to say to me concerns the play?

Lorraine   Of course it does.

Ray   In that case it is only right that the author should be present.

Lorraine   Very well. (*Offering them a cigarette box.*) I haven't got a light.

Ray   I have. (*He lights cigarettes for all three of them.*)

Lorraine   I merely want to ask you a question.

Ray   Fire away.

Lorraine   It concerns my friend Marion Blake.

Ray   Yes. I thought it might.

Lorraine   I do not as a rule listen to rumours and gossip in the theatre, but in this particular case I have been unable to avoid it.

Ray   Which specific rumours and gossip have you been unable to avoid?

Lorraine   The rumour (*she takes off her dark glasses*) that Carole Wylde has been sent for from London to replace Marion.

Ray   Correct. She has. I'm giving Marion a fortnight's notice.

Lorraine (*to* **Bryan**)   And are you in agreement with this drastic, last-minute change to the cast of your play?

Ray   The decision was mine, Lorraine. Bryan had nothing to do with it.

Lorraine   You mean that you didn't consult him any more than you have consulted me?

Ray   Certainly I consulted him. He is the author and has a right to be consulted.

Lorraine   Meaning that I have not?

Ray   The casting of the play is the business of the director and the author. It is of no concern to the actors.

Lorraine   I have news for you, Ray. The casting of the play concerns me very deeply.

A brief pause.

I wonder if you realise what the effort of creating a new part means to someone like me. After all, you are still – from the point of view of professional experience – fairly young in the theatre. For me, Ray, it is the be-all and end-all of my life. But I can't concentrate, I can't – how shall I put it? – be truly myself unless I am happy and relaxed and know that my director is on my side, rooting for me, willing me to succeed.

Ray   Are you accusing me of lack of consideration as a director?

Lorraine   I'm not accusing you of anything. I'm not blaming you for anything. I know you were in the War, and war can do terrible things to people's minds. (**Ray** *goes to speak but she cuts him off.*) I merely want to state my case. I shall be only too pleased to listen to whatever you have to say afterwards.

Ray   Very well. (*With a trace of irony.*) State away.

Lorraine   My case is this. I am lonely and frightened and completely bewildered.

Ray   Why?

Lorraine   Because I don't know what I'm supposed to have *done*! During the first few weeks of rehearsal we were close, you and I. We were growing day by day to like each other and respect each other more. But very gradually, everything seemed to change. I put out my hand trustingly as a comrade for your help and support when the path was difficult, and you were no longer there. You had withdrawn. I'd watch you and Tony – and Bryan too (*she shoots* **Bryan** *a reproachful look*) – come into the theatre, and go out of the theatre. I sometimes heard you laughing together in the stalls. I know how amusing Tony can be, and I daresay I was the butt of many of your jokes. (**Bryan** *tries to protest, but she ploughs on.*) The fact is, I was shut out, left stumbling along in the dark alone. I tried to reason with myself, to tell myself that it was all my imagination and silliness, but it wasn't and I knew it wasn't. My instincts never lie to me, and I am too honest with myself not to face the truth at all times, however unpleasant it may be. Why did you change towards me, Ray? Was it my fault? What did I do? What did I say? Was I uncooperative? Did I offend you in some way? If I did I swear it was unintentional. For God's sake, tell me, and let's make an end of it.

Tears spring to her eyes, but she dashes them away with the back of her hand. She rises to her feet, and her voice takes on a stronger, deeper note.

Don't you understand? Are you both so blind and lacking in perception that you don't realise one thing, and that is that *I love this play*. I have lived with it for weeks, for months in fact, ever since I first read it. It has been part of me night and day, waking and sleeping. And now, because of something strange, something sinister beyond my comprehension, I have lost my way to it, I can't do it – I can't, I can't, I can't!

She sinks down sobbing on to the stool in front of her dressing table. **Bryan** *is appalled by what he has heard. He rushes over to her.*

Bryan   Don't cry like that, Lorraine. Please don't cry. You're wonderful in the part – far, far more wonderful than I ever hoped anyone could ever be. Please don't be upset.

Lorraine *seizes his hand and presses her wet face against it.*

Lorraine (*brokenly*)   Thank you, Bryan. Thank you for at least trying to understand.

Ray *takes another cigarette from his case and calmly lights it.*

Ray   Is that all?

Bryan's *blood congeals at the coldness of* **Ray**'s *voice. He feels a tremor go through* **Lorraine**.

Lorraine (*lifting her head and looking* **Ray** *in the eye*)   Yes. That's all.

Ray   Are you sure you've been entirely honest in this – this 'case' you've presented?

Lorraine   Absolutely honest. But I realise already, only too clearly, that you haven't believed me.

Ray   Dead right. Not a bloody word.

Lorraine   I see. (*She rises with dignity.*) Then there is nothing more to be said.

Ray   On the contrary. (*He advances towards her and, quailing a little, she sits down again.*) There is a great deal more to be said.

Bryan   For God's sake, Ray, let's not go on about it any more. Let's finish the rehearsal.

Ray (*ferociously*)   Shut up! (*He turns back to* **Lorraine**.) You graciously said a little while ago that you would be only too pleased to listen to whatever I had to say afterwards. In that, as in everything else you have said, you were inaccurate. You will not be at all pleased to listen to what I have to say. Never, in all my limited experience of the theatre, have I seen such an inept, soggy and insincere performance as the one you have just given in this dressing room. Every gesture and every intonation was ham and false as hell, and, if I may say so, your improvised script was lousy. You are *not* lonely or lost or bewildered. You are *not* honest with yourself or with anybody else – you never have been, and you never will be. You don't give a damn whether I've changed towards you or not. All you're upset about is that you have been thwarted, denied your own way over a comparative triviality, and that is more than your overblown ego can stand.

Lorraine   Stop! I forbid you to say another word –

Ray (*mowing her down*)   You sent for me because you wanted a nice satisfying scene, ending up with all of us in tears and me comforting you and telling you that you are the most glorious, God-given genius the theatre has ever known. Then we should have billed and cooed our way through the rest of the rehearsal – which, incidentally, you need just as much as the rest of the cast (**Lorraine** *lets out an involuntary moan*) – and once firmly established on a nauseating kiss-and-be-friends basis, you would immediately have set to work again, insidiously and unscrupulously, to win back the point that you lost at the outset, namely that Marion should continue playing Stella, a part for which she is too old and entirely unsuited. It isn't even that she's bad. I can forgive a bad actress, and occasionally coax her into being a good one. But no. That poor, overpaid repertory hack is worse than bad; she's thoroughly and appallingly competent. There's no cheap technical trick that she doesn't know and use with sickening precision. No prayers, no exhortations, no carefully phrased explanations will budge her inner conviction that she knows how to do it, and what is so macabre is that she's right. She does know how to do it. But she knows how to do it *wrong* – she has always known how to do it wrong! In this particular part she is sweet, tolerant, understanding and lethal. She's a bloody murderess – she kills the character and the play stone dead with the first line she utters. And yet, Lorraine, you love her. Of course you love her! Any star would love Marion Blake: she's a megalomaniac's dream. She's a monumental bum-crawler, her clothes are catastrophic and she makes tea at matinées. But that isn't enough for me! All I ask is a decent, hard-working actress who can take direction and give proper value to the play – yes? The play you claim to love? – and the woods are full of them. One glance through *Spotlight* and I could find a dozen who would play the part perfectly. Yet here I am, landed with this superannuated, clacking soubrette because she offers you no challenge and no competition. You've wanted her in the cast from the first for one reason and one reason only, because she's a good foil to you and is shrewd enough to allow herself to be your offstage toady and bottle washer!

Lorraine (*shaking with fury*)   How dare you! How dare you speak to me like that! Get out of this room!

She rises impressively, but **Ray** *pushes her down again on to the stool. She makes an attempt to strike his hand away, but misses. He towers over her threateningly, shouting violently.*

Ray   Keep quiet! I haven't finished!

Lorraine (*screaming*)   Get out! Get out! Get out!

In a frenzy of rage, she jumps up and smacks his face so hard that he staggers back and falls on to the chaise longue. **Bryan**, *who is completely traumatised, makes a movement to intervene, but she elbows him out of the way and advances until she is standing over* **Ray**, *mascara running, hair tumbling down, eyes blazing.*

(*Spitting the words venomously into his face.*) I'll teach you to insult me in my own dressing room, you tawdry, fifth-rate amateur. Most brilliant, dynamic new director, my arse! Do you think I haven't met your sort before, camping in and out of the theatre with your giggling boyfriends? Who the hell gave you the right to throw your weight about and attempt to tell experienced actors what to do and what not to do? Go and peddle your insipid artsy-craftsy theories to some cheap summer repertory theatre where they'll be properly appreciated. Go and do *Uncle Vanya* in drapes at Birkenhead! Go and breathe new life into *Coriolanus* at the Cotswold Festival of Dramatic Art, but get out of my sight!

At this moment, the door bursts open to admit **Marion**, *who hurtles into the room, attired in an Alice-blue satin wrapper, with some cheesecloth swathed round her head and carrying a tortoiseshell hairbrush. With a piercing cry, she throws herself between* **Ray** *and* **Lorraine**.

Marion   Don't, don't, don't! The whole theatre can hear you, and I love you both!

Marion flings her arms round **Lorraine***, who shoves her away.*
Ray*, seething with rage, pulls himself to his feet.*

Ray (*icily*)   That, Marion, is entirely irrelevant. You're fired anyway!

He strides out of the room, slamming the door after him.

Blackout. Music crashes in.

Scene Three

As the music segues to a more wistful, lyrical tune, the lights come up to reveal the dressing room as it appears the following night. The first performance is coming to an end. The room is filled with lavish baskets and bouquets of flowers, first night cards, telegrams and presents.

Nora *is sitting on the* chaise longue*, doing her knitting. After a few moments,* **Bryan** *comes down the corridor, dressed in black tie, and puts his head round the door.*

Bryan   Do you mind if I come and join you, Nora? I just can't sit still any longer. Too nervous.

Nora   'Course you can – come and sit down.

He comes into the room, shuts the door and sits on the stool.

Help yourself to a cigarette.

Bryan (*taking one*)   Thanks.

Nora   Match?

Bryan   I've got a lighter, thank you.

He lights his cigarette and takes out his notebook. He writes a couple of lines in silence, while **Nora** *gets on with her knitting. Then he puts his pen down.*

I hate first nights, don't you?

Nora   I've been through too many in my time to bother about them any more.

Bryan   I envy you.

Nora   I was with old Naomi Calvin for seven years. She used to be sick in the basin before each act, regular as clockwork.

Bryan   I never saw her, I'm sorry to say. Was she wonderful?

Nora   All right. Especially when she had to come to a sticky end. She could die better than anyone in the business. Best thing she ever did, to my mind, was *Call Back the Years*. Her death throes put an extra eight minutes on the running time, but the public were mad about her.

Bryan   You don't seem to be very impressed by our leading ladies, Nora.

Nora   I've seen too many of them at close quarters. When it comes down to it they're not so different from anyone else.

Bryan   They must have a sort of extra something, though, otherwise they wouldn't be stars.

Nora   If you ask me, the extra something they've got is conceit. Still, I'd rather have Miss Barrie, with all her carryings-on, than one of the simple so-called unaffected ones.

Bryan   Would you really?

Nora   Well, they're so set on being folksy and human and unspoilt by their great success that they get all slummocky.

Bryan *doesn't understand the term.*

Nora   Oh, you know, turning up at the theatre in slacks
and sweaters, with scarves over their heads, like a lot of
factory hands. At least Miss Barrie has the sense to behave
like the genuine article. You don't see her slouching about
looking grubby, with her hair all over the shop.

Bryan   No, you certainly don't.

Nora   When she goes out of that stage door every night
after the show she looks like a million dollars. Not flashy,
mind you, but stylish. How's she doing tonight?

Bryan   Spellbinding – never seen her better. Every
gesture, every movement: perfection . . . I still can't really
believe that she agreed to do my play. After all, people
normally think of her playing comic parts.

Nora   Oh yes. There's no one to touch her at that.

Bryan   So why did she agree to do this, do you think?

Nora   They're all the same. Once they get set in one line
of business, they immediately want to try their hand at
something else. Plus she'd had a bit of a lean patch, to tell
you the honest. And there was a nasty tax bill looming, I
believe. And, of course, she didn't have a gentleman at the
time, and I think that always makes her restless.

While **Bryan** *is trying to take this in, there's a knock at the door.*

Nora   Come in.

Gerald *appears, in costume and smoking his pipe.*

Gerald (*to* **Bryan**)   Ah-ha! Thought I saw you sneaking
through the pass door. How d'you reckon it's going, dear
fellow?

Bryan   Wonderfully. I just couldn't stand the tension any
longer.

Gerald *hovers, fishing for a compliment.*

Bryan   But you're on great form, Gerald. Lots of
marvellous new things.

Gerald Yes, yes, they seem to be liking it. (*He comes in and shuts the door.*) Of course they're missing all the finer points. That bit when I'm playing with the paper knife. Went for nothing. In London, you see, they'll be on to that. How are you, Nora?

Nora Not too bad, thank you, Mr Wentworth.

Gerald Jolly good. (*Wandering round the room.*) Of course, that's really my best act now. The part goes to pieces in Act Three. (*Remembering who he's talking to.*) Not that it's your fault, dear chap. I know that Lorraine and Ray bullied you into rewriting the end of the play, but if you want my candid opinion, it was better as it was. Of course I see Lorraine's point. If we'd played the original version she'd have been offstage committing suicide for the last ten minutes of the play. As it is, she finishes on the stage by herself with the telephone. And I'm not saying that she doesn't do it beautifully. Nobody can smile through her tears better than she can. After all, she made her first great success in *Sheila Goes Away* doing precisely the same scene – not as well written, of course, but essentially the same – and she's been doing it in different ways ever since. Did you ever see her in *Winter Wind* at the Strand?

Bryan I don't think I was born then.

Gerald Pity. Well, that was more or less the identical situation all over again. Except that there was no telephone on account of it being Victorian.

Bryan *lets out a barely audible groan, and puts his head in his hands.*

Gerald You all right, m'dear?

Bryan (*muffled*) Fine.

Gerald Good show. (*Playing as much to* **Nora** *as to* **Bryan** *now.*) But there she was, crinoline and all, giving up her lover and going back to her husband with a wistful smile. You've never read such notices. Old Agate – now he's what I call a critic – he compared her with that French actress there was such a hullabaloo about. Not Bernhardt, I think. (*He smiles affably*.) Must have been the other one. (*Scrutinising his teeth in the mirror*.) She was a touch slow in the first act tonight, I thought. But she always takes her time to build. I've played with her enough times to know all her funny little ways. She'll get there in a week or two. (*Returning to the door*.) Anyhow, better get back. Just acknowledge the ovation, then we can all bugger off for a small Wincarnis. So long.

He exits. **Nora** *puts down her knitting and tidies some clothes on to hangers.*

Nora   I better go down too – she likes me to be in the wings when she comes off. Won't you be taking a bow then, dear?

Bryan (*rallying*)   No, Mr Malcolm didn't want us to get caught up in Miss Barrie's curtain speech.

Nora   Very wise. If it's a good night she tends to go on a bit, thanking everyone under the sun, declaring it's the happiest night of her life, blowing kisses. I reckon tonight could be a kiss-blower. Back in a tick.

Nora *exits.* **Bryan** *looks round the room listlessly, examining the cards and flowers, as if seeing it all for the first time. Suddenly,* **Ray** *and* **Tony** *appear, both in evening dress.* **Tony**'s *notepad is sticking out of his pocket.*

Ray   Ah, here you are!

Bryan (*checking his watch*)   It's not over, is it?

Ray (*flinging himself on to the* chaise longue)   No, but I've had enough for one night. Open the champers, Tony – we should have time for a glass before she gets down.

Tony (*opening one of the bottles on the dressing table*)   She hasn't started her curtain speech yet. If you hurry you could probably fit in a mastoid operation and a perm.

Bryan   Are you pleased with the way it went, Ray?

Ray   Not bad, all things considered. Lots of tightening to do. Have you got my notes, Tony?

Tony   They're scorching the lining of my pocket. (*He pours out the champagne.*)

Bryan (*almost impatient*)   'All things considered'? It's a miracle she went on after last night.

Ray (*airily*)   Oh no, there was never any question of her not going on.

Tony   It'd be breach of contract, you see.

Bryan   I thought she'd claim she was ill.

Tony   You need a doctor's certificate for that.

Ray   Come on, she's hardly going to give up the best part she's had in twenty years.

Bryan   Well, now you put it like that . . . (*Pointedly.*) How was the last scene going?

Ray   It works very well.

Bryan   Gerald seems to have got hold of the idea that Lorraine finishes every play with a soliloquy like that.

Tony   Yes. (*Unsentimentally.*) That's why I suggested it.

Ray   The only difference was that tonight the lights over the fireplace went on the blink.

Tony (*handing out the drinks*)   I still think it was the chief electrician giving Marion her notice in Morse code.

Bryan (*determined not to lose his temper*)   You've got to hand it to Marion – she is a trouper. How could anyone act like that with unemployment lurking round the corner?

Ray   It's precisely because she acts like that that unemployment *is* lurking round the corner.

Bryan   Aren't you nervous about facing Lorraine? What do you think's going to happen?

Ray (*deliberately obtuse*)   When?

Bryan   When she comes in and finds us all lolling around in her dressing room drinking her champagne. What happens if she refuses to speak to you?

Ray   Nothing much, I suppose. Maybe *I'll* speak to *her*. Cheers!

Bryan (*half-heartedly*)   Cheers.

Tony   Cheers! Oh I do so love a family reunion.

We can now hear the distant sound of applause from the auditorium. After relishing this for a second or two, **Bryan** *shuts the door and the applause cuts out.*

Bryan   Wouldn't it save a lot of trouble if you gave in gracefully and didn't fire Marion?

Ray   Christ! Whose side are you on? I'm not giving in to blackmail.

Bryan   Blackmail?

Ray   That's what it's all about. Lorraine is acting up like this on the assumption that she's indispensible. It's one of the routine delusions of stardom.

Tony   The whole thing is primarily biological.

Bryan   Don't be silly.

Tony   It's true. It began way back in the beginning of the world when the Almighty, for reasons best known to Himself, arranged that ladies should be constructed differently from gentlemen.

Bryan   For goodness' sake!

Tony   All temperamental scenes made by all temperamental female stars since the theatre was first invented have been based on that inescapable fact.

Ray   Correct.

Tony   It isn't, of course, their fault entirely. It's drummed into their fluffy little heads from infancy, through adolescence and on into adult life that they possess something unique and infinitely precious, something that every man they meet desires more than anything else. The dawning realisation that, in the theatrical profession at least, this comforting conviction isn't always true, flings them into paroxysms of fury and frustration. They hate the men who do want them and the men who don't, and they hate each other profoundly and mercilessly.

Bryan   That's an absurd generalisation and you both know it. The truth is that the theatre is run by a small clique of pampered, puffed-up, self-serving men. Where would they be without actresses like Lorraine Barrie? I'll tell you – they'd be out of a job. I'd never have had my play produced without her. I'm under no illusion. She's the one that the public pays to see. But, for some reason, that really irks you, doesn't it? Why not admit it? The simple fact is that you just don't like women.

Tony   Don't be silly, dear, we adore women.

Ray   Although not, I grant you, in what is known as 'that way'.

Tony   Some of our best friends are women though, aren't they?

Ray   Yes – true.

Tony   And they're a damn sight more loyal and sweet to us than most of our male chums. Above all, I love great big diamond-studded glamour stars; they fascinate me.

Ray   And as for Lorraine, I *dote* on all her little tricks and carryings-on, her magnificent dishonesty, her eternal gullibility . . .

Tony   So it's no use accusing us in that prim, disapproving voice of not liking women, because it just doesn't make sense. Nobody can love the theatre without liking women.

They are the most fascinating, unpredictable and exciting
part of it.

Beat.·

Ray   But I'm damned if I'm going to let her think she's
won, after my famous victory last night.

Bryan (*angry now*)   Why should there be winners and
losers? It's so childish. We're putting on a play, not fighting
a bloody war. Why can't people in the theatre behave like
normal human beings?

Ray   Because there wouldn't be a theatre if they did.

Suddenly **Lorraine** *walks into the room, taking off her earrings.
She's radiant. She stops in her tracks when she sees the three men.*
Nora *follows her in, and tactfully goes over to the clothes rail.*
Lorraine *looks at* **Ray**, *who is at the other end of the room. Silence.
Eventually, the tension is broken by* **Bryan**, *who goes across to her.*

Bryan   You were marvellous, Lorraine, absolutely
marvellous. You've never given such a performance. It was
magnificent.

Lorraine (*wistfully*)   Thank you. Dear Bryan. (*She kisses
him.*)

Bryan   The audience adored you.

Lorraine   A lot of cod's heads. I said we should have
opened in Edinburgh.

Bryan   It was the most thrilling night of my life.

Lorraine   You'll have many more, of that I'm certain.
Just wait and see. (**Nora** *exits, taking a dress on a hanger with her.*
Lorraine *turns to* **Ray**; *silence.*) Well?

Ray (*holding her gaze unblinkingly*)   Well?

Tony   Well! (*Grabbing hold of* **Bryan**.) We're just running
away quietly to start a new life together. But if we change
our minds we'll see you for supper at the Midland Hotel in
half an hour.

Tony *swipes the bottle of champagne and drags* **Bryan** *out.*
Lorraine *and* **Ray** *continue to stare each other out.*

Lorraine (*pointedly*)   Were you pleased with me? Was I a good girl?

Ray (*steadfastly refusing to throw her even a scrap of praise*)   What did *you* think? Didn't you feel the audience's reaction?

Lorraine   Of course.

Ray   Good.

Lorraine (*hungry for his praise*)   But it was you that I was thinking about, Ray, all through the evening. I tried to remember everything you'd told me. I know I went a bit overboard in the letter scene, but it won't happen again, I promise.

Ray (*relenting at last, and what he says is sincere*)   You were beyond praise.

Lorraine   You didn't think so last night.

Ray   Last night I vowed never to speak to you again. But that was last night. What matters is that you've proved me right. I always said you were a bloody good actress.

Lorraine   It's a bloody good part.

Ray   Yes. But no one else could bring to it your peculiar magic.

Lorraine *walks slowly towards him, but we can't tell what she's thinking.* **Ray** *doesn't budge an inch. At last she reaches him. Suddenly she kisses him full on the lips, and then takes him in her arms, holding on to him tight. The lights close in on them.*

Scene Four

The stage management strike the furniture, and we are back on the empty stage again, after the performance of Dark Heritage. **Bryan** *and* **Tony** *wander on to the stage, champagne flutes in hand, bow ties* *undone.* **Bryan** *is on his third glass and slightly high. He looks out into the vast auditorium and sighs.*

Bryan   How many first nights has this theatre seen, I wonder?

Tony (*raising his glass*)   The Palace, Manchester, and all who play in her! (*They drink.*)

Bryan   Did you know that Lorraine first appeared here when she was seven years old?

Tony   When the hell was that?

Bryan   1899. There's a playbill in the Circle Bar. *The Winter's Tale.* For Two Nights Only.

Tony (*counting on his fingers*)   So that makes her . . .

Bryan   Don't – it's rude to count.

He smiles to himself and walks away along the edge of the footlights.

Gerald's quite wrong, you know: the audience picked up on everything. Are they always that receptive here?

Tony   I think they're like audiences anywhere.

Bryan   Yes; If you put on plays that tackle serious themes head-on –

Tony   People will stay away in droves.

Bryan   What?!

Tony   It's true! I'm not denying that your little play tells us lots of clever things; of course it does, and that's lovely. But no: people go to the theatre to be entertained. So don't stop writing.

Bryan (*brandishing his notebook*)   I've already made notes for my next play.

Tony   Very good!

Bryan   You lot have provided me with some pretty good copy.

Tony (*smiling*)   And you really don't mind going through all this again?

Bryan   You needn't worry about me.

Tony   Oh but I do, I do. I've lain awake at night, tormented by your starry-eyed innocence.

Bryan (*going over and holding out his glass*)   You're a hopeless case, Tony.

Tony (*pouring champagne*)   You're quite right. There's no point talking to me seriously about anything. Apart from topics you always seem so eager to avoid.

Bryan (*with a long-suffering smile*)   Such as?

Tony   Oh, I don't know – sex? Come on, you can tell me, you *must* be in love with someone. Who is it? Not Ray – he's spoken for; and please God not Lorraine. It would make her even more conceited.

Bryan   Why on earth do you all think she's conceited? I don't think she is at all. She's Lorraine Barrie – isn't that enough?

Tony   It's more than enough. It is unequivocally and eternally right. But there's something you're forgetting.

Bryan   Yes?

Tony   Something which alone makes her unassailable.

Bryan   Oh no, I was leaving that till last. Her talent. That's her one reality, and it's rock solid. Apart from that, she has nothing that thousands of other women don't possess to a far greater degree.

He opens his notebook, finds the relevant page and reads.

'Her looks are little more than attractively adequate. She's virtually illiterate; her conversation is amusing but empty. She loves nobody, and nobody loves her. Occasionally they may think they do; occasionally she may think she does, but there's no truth in it. Her whole life is passed in a sort of hermetically sealed projection room watching her own rushes.' (*He looks up at* **Tony**.) That's rather good, isn't it?

Tony   Go on.

Bryan   'She can be alluring, forbidding, very grand, utterly simple, kind, cruel, – it all depends what performance she's putting on for herself at that moment. Who she really is, nobody knows – least of all herself.'

He lowers his book. The lights slowly begin to fade until by the end of his speech, **Bryan**'s *face alone is illuminated by a pin spot.*

But then . . . you pay your money at the box office and you go in and watch her on a matinée day with a dull audience, in a bad play with the fortnight's notice up on the board, and the house half full, and suddenly you are aware that you are in the presence of something very great indeed – something abstract, that is beyond definition and beyond praise. Quality – star quality. It's there as strongly in comedy as in tragedy, magical and unmistakable, and the hair will rise on the back of your neck, chills will swirl up and down your spine and you will solemnly bless the day that you were born . . .

As he finishes speaking, applause breaks in and **Lorraine** *is revealed centre stage. She has her back to us and is taking her curtain call. A row of footlights upstage shines brightly up at her and a brilliant white spotlight is trained on her from above. The clapping from the black void grows louder.* **Tony** *and* **Bryan**, *who are standing at either side of the stage, look up at* **Lorraine** *from the shadows. As the ovation reaches its peak, the sound cuts out.* **Lorraine** *stands frozen in the limelight. Silence for a few seconds, and then –*

Blackout.

Methuen Modern Plays

include work by

Jean Anouilh
John Arden
Margaretta D'Arcy
Peter Barnes
Sebastian Barry
Brendan Behan
Dermot Bolger
Edward Bond
Bertolt Brecht
Howard Brenton
Anthony Burgess
Simon Burke
Jim Cartwright
Caryl Churchill
Noël Coward
Lucinda Coxon
Sarah Daniels
Nick Darke
Nick Dear
Shelagh Delaney
David Edgar
David Eldridge
Dario Fo
Michael Frayn
John Godber
Paul Godfrey
David Greig
John Guare
Peter Handke
David Harrower
Jonathan Harvey
Iain Heggie
Declan Hughes
Terry Johnson
Sarah Kane
Charlotte Keatley
Barrie Keeffe
Howard Korder

Robert Lepage
Stephen Lowe
Doug Lucie
Martin McDonagh
John McGrath
Terrence McNally
David Mamet
Patrick Marber
Arthur Miller
Mtwa, Ngema & Simon
Tom Murphy
Phyllis Nagy
Peter Nichols
Joseph O'Connor
Joe Orton
Louise Page
Joe Penhall
Luigi Pirandello
Stephen Poliakoff
Franca Rame
Mark Ravenhill
Philip Ridley
Reginald Rose
David Rudkin
Willy Russell
Jean-Paul Sartre
Sam Shepard
Wole Soyinka
Shelagh Stephenson
C. P. Taylor
Theatre de Complicite
Theatre Workshop
Sue Townsend
Judy Upton
Timberlake Wertenbaker
Roy Williams
Victoria Wood

Methuen Contemporary Dramatists

include

Peter Barnes (three volumes)
Sebastian Barry
Edward Bond (six volumes)
Howard Brenton
  (two volumes)
Richard Cameron
Jim Cartwright
Caryl Churchill (two volumes)
Sarah Daniels (two volumes)
Nick Darke
David Edgar (three volumes)
Ben Elton
Dario Fo (two volumes)
Michael Frayn (two volumes)
Paul Godfrey
John Guare
Peter Handke
Jonathan Harvey
Declan Hughes
Terry Johnson (two volumes)
Bernard-Marie Koltès
David Lan
Bryony Lavery
Doug Lucie
David Mamet (three volumes)

Martin McDonagh
Duncan McLean
Anthony Minghella
  (two volumes)
Tom Murphy (four volumes)
Phyllis Nagy
Anthony Nielsen
Philip Osment
Louise Page
Joe Penhall
Stephen Poliakoff
  (three volumes)
Christina Reid
Philip Ridley
Willy Russell
Ntozake Shange
Sam Shepard (two volumes)
Wole Soyinka (two volumes)
David Storey (three volumes)
Sue Townsend
Michel Vinaver (two volumes)
Michael Wilcox
David Wood (two volumes)
Victoria Wood

Methuen World Classics

include

Jean Anouilh (two volumes)
John Arden (two volumes)
Arden & D'Arcy
Brendan Behan
Aphra Behn
Bertolt Brecht (six volumes)
Büchner
Bulgakov
Calderón
Čapek
Anton Chekhov
Noël Coward (seven volumes)
Eduardo De Filippo
Max Frisch
John Galsworthy
Gogol
Gorky
Harley Granville Barker
  (two volumes)
Henrik Ibsen (six volumes)
Lorca (three volumes)

Marivaux
Mustapha Matura
David Mercer (two volumes)
Arthur Miller (five volumes)
Molière
Musset
Peter Nichols (two volumes)
Clifford Odets
Joe Orton
A. W. Pinero
Luigi Pirandello
Terence Rattigan
  (two volumes)
W. Somerset Maugham
  (two volumes)
August Strindberg
  (three volumes)
J. M. Synge
Ramón del Valle-Inclán
Frank Wedekind
Oscar Wilde

Methuen Student Editions

A SELECTED LIST OF
METHUEN MODERN PLAYS

CLOSER	Patrick Marber	£6.99
THE BEAUTY QUEEN OF LEENANE	Martin McDonagh	£6.99
A SKULL IN CONNEMARA	Martin McDonagh	£6.99
THE LONESOME WEST	Martin McDonagh	£6.99
THE CRIPPLE OF INISHMAAN	Martin McDonagh	£6.99
THE STEWARD OF CHRISTENDOM	Sebastian Barry	£6.99
SHOPPING AND F***ING	Mark Ravenhill	£6.99
FAUST (FAUST IS DEAD)	Mark Ravenhill	£5.99
COPENHAGEN	Michael Frayn	£6.99
POLYGRAPH	Robert Lepage and Marie Brassard	£6.99
BEAUTIFUL THING	Jonathan Harvey	£6.99
MEMORY OF WATER & FIVE KINDS OF SILENCE	Shelagh Stephenson	£7.99
WISHBONES	Lucinda Coxton	£6.99
BONDAGERS & THE STRAW CHAIR	Sue Glover	£9.99
SOME VOICES & PALE HORSE	Joe Penhall	£7.99
KNIVES IN HENS	David Harrower	£6.99
BOYS LIFE & SEARCH AND DESTROY	Howard Korder	£8.99
THE LIGHTS	Howard Korder	£6.99
SERVING IT UP & A WEEK WITH TONY	David Eldridge	£8.99
INSIDE TRADING	Malcolm Bradbury	£6.99
MASTERCLASS	Terence McNally	£5.99
EUROPE & THE ARCHITECT	David Greig	£7.99
BLUE MURDER	Peter Nichols	£6.99
BLASTED & PHAEDRA'S LOVE	Sarah Kane	£7.99

* All Methuen Drama books are available through mail order or from your local bookshop. Please send cheque/eurocheque/postal order (sterling only) Access, Visa, Mastercard, Diners Card, Switch or Amex.

Expiry Date: .... Signature: ....

Please allow 75 pence per book for post and packing U.K.
Overseas customers please allow £1.00 per copy for post and packing.

ALL ORDERS TO:
Methuen Books, Books by Post, TBS Limited, The Book Service, Colchester Road, Frating Green, Colchester, Essex CO7 7DW.

NAME ....

ADDRESS ....

....

....

Please allow 28 days for delivery. Please tick box if you do not wish to receive any additional information

Prices and availability subject to change without notice.

For a complete catalogue of Methuen Drama titles
write to:

Methuen Drama
215 Vauxhall Bridge Road
London SW1V 1EJ

or you can visit our website at:

www.methuen.co.uk